MW01485781

THE
ELDER CARE
PLAYBOOK

HOW TO ORGANIZE CARE
FOR YOUR AGING LOVED ONE

PETRA WEGGEL

MOKUPUNI PUBLISHING LLC

HAIKU, HAWAII

The Elder Care Playbook is a work of nonfiction.
Some identifying details have been changed.

Book & Cover Design, Drawings by Petra Weggel

Published in the United States by Mokupuni Publishing LLC

Library of Congress Cataloging Number: 2021901733

First Edition

Print ISBN: 978-1-7363602-0-0
eBook ISBN: ISBN: 978-1-7363602-1-7

For ordering information visit: theeldercareplaybook.com

Printed in the United States of America

In loving memory of my brother, who always
looked at the bright side of life and my dad,
whose outgoing personality influenced me in so many ways.

And to my mom,
she taught me kindness and patience – lots of patience.

"Life is what happens
when you are busy making plans."

— *John Lennon*

Contents

TIME TO GET MOVING

MIND YOURSELF

It is incredibly stressful to witness the decline of an aging loved one while at the same time thinking about your own mounting responsibilities. You probably have your own job, a family or significant other, and bills that are piling up. To deal with all of that while also knowing your parent's affairs are a mess can leave you feeling lost and hopeless. If you're like I was, you won't even know where to begin...

Introduction

The Purpose of This Book

I want to start this book by telling you I am not a geriatric care professional. I'm simply the daughter of a 92-year-old woman who lives thousands of miles away. She had always wanted to age in her own home for as long as possible. It was only when her day-to-day safety became a question that she was moved into a nursing home.

Like most Americans, I understood why it was important to plan for the future. And, like most families, I didn't actually have any plan in place when the real problems started to be obvious. But, by flying by the seat of my pants and using the organizational skills I had gained as a small business owner, I managed to set up a situation that is safe and comfortable for my mother while also manageable for me. Against all odds I found a way to ensure a meaningful and caring future for the woman who raised me. Now I want to help others do the same.

As our loved ones get older, they will naturally become more fragile. As they become needier – and as lingering medical issues progress – adult children and other close relatives may begin to live in a constant state of worry. We start to agonize over what could happen. In an ideal world we would be living close to our aging folks. We would have functioning family relationships, unlimited funds, and the time to support and pamper our parents (and ourselves) until they passed on. Unfortunately, that's not the reality in most cases.

If you're reading this book, it's likely your family dynamics are more on the "complicated" side. Money is probably tight, and time even tighter. You might live in a different state or country than your aging relative. You could even be a busy parent with a demanding job and a full life. If that's the case, what do you do when shit happens? What comes next when a crisis occurs and suddenly the caregiver roles are reversed? Do you sacrifice the career you've worked so hard for? Can you leave your own family? Won't your kids need you?

It's simply not feasible for many of us to become full-time caregivers. If that's the situation you have found yourself in, this book is for you. It's written for those who cannot care for an aging parent or a younger disabled one. And it's for those who can't pack up, move closer, or give up their lives for reasons that are personal, professional, or financial. It's for everyone like me in the sandwich generation who can't bring a parent home to live with them but still wants to know they'll be cared for.

What I want you to know, right from the start, is that you don't have to be physically present to do your part. You can become a *care organizer*, like I did, while still working and attending to your life.

There is no doubt that living close by an aging loved one can give a big boost to their quality of life while providing you with peace of mind. One of the hardest things about being away from an older parent or relative is not being able to help out quickly when unexpected situations arise. It doesn't take a huge emergency to set off your sense of worry. What would be easy for a younger person to deal with can seem like a mountain of trouble for an aging adult. In those moments your presence can make a huge difference – for yourself and your loved one.

In the real world, though, some relationships can be tricky and life often gets in the way. Even if you have the best intentions, volunteering your own time and abandoning other priorities can cause great stress for yourself and your family. You have to be careful about what you commit to. While it might not be perfect, organizing care from a distance can still be valuable... and much less overwhelming.

All we really want for our aging loved ones is happiness, good health, and to know they can live the remainder of their lives in comfort and dignity. My goal for this book is to help you accomplish that for yourself and your parent or loved one, even if you have circumstances that are less than ideal. I'm going to help you make the process of organizing care less daunting and more manageable.

Along the way, I'm going to give you lots of useful ideas and checklists so you can stay focused and keep your sanity. I will also be sharing my own experiences so you can understand what led me to break this process down. You'll learn why you have to put your own well-being first, and coping methods to deal with frustration, guilt, and helplessness. I want you to think of this book as not only a tool for planning, but also your inspirational support manual. You really can find time for yourself, avoid burnout, *and* help the person you care about at the same time.

Please note that I'll be using terms like *senior, elder, and elderly* throughout the coming chapters. While we may never agree on who is actually elderly based on age, I'm using these words (for lack of a better alternative) to describe someone who is frail, lacking physical strength, or suffering from declining cognitive abilities. In this context, "elderly" means showing the typical symptoms associated with age, illness, or accident. Keep in mind that your loved one may not be a parent; they could be a younger person struggling with the same issues. In fact, someone you care about may qualify, even temporarily, after hospitalization or some other setback.

Also know that I don't claim this book to be a comprehensive text on the subject of senior care or caregiving. That would be too presumptuous. It would be virtually impossible for me to give you inclusive, step-by-step directions on the topic of helping your loved one, particularly when you consider how many potential medical, personal, or financial circumstances could be involved. Each situation is different, and every family dynamic is unique. Things will change from one case to the next. Additionally, legal and health care systems vary from one state or country to another.

While I can't claim to give you everything, what I *can* do is tell you many aspects of organizing care remain the same no matter where you are in relation to the person you care for. What worked for my parents' situation in Germany may never work for you here in the US or wherever you are, but the concerns are largely the same. The hurdles I had to overcome over the past ten years could have applied to anyone in my generation across the world. I'm going to share those with you, along with everything I learned along the way. My hope is that my story might inspire and guide anyone out there facing the same senior care issues, whether now or in the foreseeable future.

I thought long and hard about the right order for the material in this book. Eventually, I came to the conclusion that there isn't a one-size-fits-all approach for diving into the subject of organizing elder care. Even though I have broken the process down into digestible chunks, where you begin ultimately depends on your own circumstances, not to mention your loved one's health issues, your relationship to each other, and your own family situation. Whether you read this book from front to back or just pick out a few chapters is entirely up to you.

Personal circumstances are going to dictate your priorities. But, if I were to give you an outline of how best to prepare yourself for your aging parent's care, it would look something like this:

1. Bring order into your life and learn good stress-management techniques.

2. Assess your loved one's situation and discuss their wishes.

3. Find out whether necessary paperwork has been prepared.

4. Gather information and documents you need so you'll have them at your fingertips at all times.

5. Find someone trustworthy to be your backup.

6. Learn all about the different senior care options.

7. Figure out what your loved one can afford and what type of

housing they prefer.

8. Shop around, narrow down the options, and make choices.

There you have it. These are the basics of early preparation. And they are all things you can tackle as quickly as today. You can begin working with them bit by bit so that later, when a situation unfolds, you're ready to do your part.

It is much, much easier to care for an aging loved one when you're prepared. However, you will never be completely off the hook. Even after your loved one's living situation has been dealt with and care has been organized, you'll need to expect the unexpected. Many players will be involved in your loved one's care – including medical professionals, personal caregivers, social workers, friends, and family members. It will be your job to orchestrate this effort in addition to playing the important role of being a personal administrator, financial manager, steady rock, and emotional backbone.

Situations will keep changing. You may discover (as I have) that one day everything will be fine and the next there will be a crisis. There may come a time when you have to step up to the task of providing support and comfort, and to be there in person to help your fragile loved one. I am going to show you how to set the stage so you can take a hiatus as needed to deal with these eventualities.

I sincerely hope you will find your own healthy way of dealing with your new situation, and that you won't feel guilty about maintaining your own life while acting as a *care organizer* instead of a *caregiver*. I also hope that the information I provide will get you organized ahead of time so you can enjoy the precious years you have with your loved one instead of worrying about the details of caring for them.

I have a model in my life: "Every Day Is a Good Day." This book is all about helping you adopt that mindset and spend each day in a way that feels meaningful instead of overwhelmed.

This book is not intended to offer legal, financial, or health care advice. Laws, costs, rules, and regulations may vary from one area to another and even within the same city.

Little did I know, when I was looking for the perfect place to enjoy my life, that the consequences wouldn't come into focus for more than twenty years.

Torn Between Two Worlds

Life Is Unpredictable

A fter a successful career and a busy life in New York City, I decided to move to Maui – some 7,500+ miles away from my homeland of Germany – to become a business owner. I've never regretted that decision. To this day I love living here. I love my work and my clients. Running my own company has been everything I hoped it would be.

Together with my wonderful partner I enjoy a comfortable life with a beautiful home and many friends. I love my work, and can always go to the beach or play tennis. It hasn't always been easy, and it took a lot of hard work to get to where I am today. Still, I wouldn't sacrifice any part of it.

For all the obvious advantages only in Hawaii, however, there are also disadvantages. The price you pay for living in a remote paradise is that you have to fly every time you want to visit family. That's true for most haoles (as the Hawaiian language describes any foreigner or foreign object introduced to the islands), and it's especially true in my case. All of my relatives live halfway around the world. Visiting them takes advanced planning and is relatively costly. That's something I accepted when I moved here.

This wasn't a big deal to me for many years until my situation changed in the blink of an eye. Out of nowhere came the news that my older brother, and only sibling, had died unexpectedly. The loss of my *big bruddah* stung, but after the shock faded it dawned on me that my role in the family was about to change. My brother had lived close to my parents, but I did not. He was significantly older and would naturally have been the one in charge of caring for them as they aged.

That plan changed in a moment and I realized the job would fall to me... even though I hadn't signed up for it.

I could tell my mom and dad were struggling with that realization as well. The natural order of things had been upset and, even though they didn't say it to my face, I could sense they were also afraid I couldn't – or maybe wouldn't – be there for them when they needed me. To be honest, I was afraid of that myself.

This wasn't about worry, it was about reality. Even then I began to  realize it would be extremely difficult for me to take care of my aging parents from such a great distance. At the same time, my business wouldn't just run itself. I depended on the income it generated, and when I wasn't present I wasn't making any money. To make matters worse, I wasn't even close to retirement. Moving to Germany was out of the question.

Relocating my parents to Hawaii wasn't an option, either. My father had suffered through repeated episodes of cardiac distress for several years. Flying was dangerous for him. My mother couldn't speak English or drive a car. It was hard to see how either of them would survive the kind of move that would be required, much less thrive. And, for what it was worth, neither of them *wanted* to live in Hawaii.

Practical and economic considerations aside, I was also worried about my personal relationship with my partner. I knew it would falter if I decided to move back to Germany, that much was already clear. With all of this floating in the air, the question that ran endlessly through my mind following my brother's death was: "How will I be taking care of my parents as they get older?" I didn't have a good answer, much less a plan. So, I did nothing and just waited.

As with all things we try to put off, my problem eventually came to me. It was during a visit to Germany. Mom was puttering away in her kitchen, as always, while Dad sat on his sofa watching TV. None of this was out of the ordinary, but I had the sense that something was wrong with the picture. Dad's favorite news show was on, but he wasn't really tuned in. Instead, he was just sitting there with a blank stare while the anchor announced the latest stories. This was very much out of character for him.

"Any interesting news?" I asked. Dad looked at me as if he were seeing me for the first time and didn't know who I was.

Over the next few days, I noticed other troubling signs. My father could talk in vivid detail about past encounters and stories from his life, but couldn't recall anything short-term. I was heartbroken and alarmed – he was showing the first signs of dementia. How fast, I wondered, was the illness going to progress? With his memory fading away and his judgment suffering, how many months or weeks would he have before all would be lost?

When I asked my mother about the situation she admitted she had noticed the changes a while ago. She hadn't said anything because she didn't want to alarm me.

I started to worry even more. I wasn't just concerned for my father, but also for my mother and their future together. Heart problems and dementia were not a good combination. It was clearly only a matter of time before he might be considered mentally unfit to make sound decisions or sign legal documents. Something had to be done. The clock was ticking and my mother confirmed that they hadn't prepared for any of the eventualities they were about to face. She didn't even know where to begin. I didn't either, but I knew I would have to figure it out before my flight back home.

It wasn't that my mother wanted to dump the whole mess on my plate. She simply didn't have the skills to tackle a problem like the one in front of her.

Dad was quite a character; this book would not be complete if I didn't describe him to you. He could strike up a conversation with just about anyone. He was outgoing, with a quick sense of humor and a habit of looking at the bright side of life. He considered himself an optimist and used to say with a big grin on his face: "Do you know what the difference is between an optimist and a pessimist? An optimist books a hotel room before going on a blind date."

As likable as Dad was, though, he was also the embodiment of *stur* – the German word for stubborn or stoic. When he set his mind to something, there was no changing it.

Like many men of his generation, Dad had taken care of all the finances and real estate-related issues, keeping most details to himself. "That's *men's* business," he would say. Mom's role was to take care of us kids and manage the household. She never had to write a check. She did not use a bank card, or even know how to access the couple's bank accounts. When she needed money he would just give her some. What she *did* do was make a hell of a pork roast with dumplings. Together, she and my father made quite a team for 66 years of marriage.

> We just never know what the future has in store for us.

Unfortunately, none of that time had prepared my mom to deal with the details of managing their home, their finances and paperwork. She certainly couldn't jump to that role for both of them. I knew it wouldn't be fair of me to expect her to handle things without help. Obviously, it was going to be up to me to gather the facts and figure out what to do next. The only question was: Would Dad hand over the reins willingly, or would he stonewall?

The clock was ticking and I had to quickly learn about the details of their life together. I needed to get on top of their finances, locate details about insurance, catalog the rental properties they owned, and so on. Otherwise there was the risk that all would be forgotten or even lost.

Without his mind and memory it would be poof... and gone forever.

When the shock of my father's situation wore off, my mind went into overdrive. There was alot that needed to get done before I had to get on the flight back home. He had good days and bad days, so I picked one of the better ones to talk with him about their future. I told him I wanted to understand his wishes and explained I would need to have a durable power of attorney signed in my name. Without it, I wouldn't be able to act on their behalf.

In response my father proudly handed me a handwritten note stating I could act on behalf of my parents. I was, shall we say, *slightly skeptical* of the legitimacy of the document. I knew it was intended to be a generous gesture from him to me, but made an attempt to convince him that consulting an attorney might be a good idea. Then, the document could be reviewed and properly drafted. But Dad refused. He was being *stur.*

While I waited for my father to come around on the issue of a lawyer, I began to gather information. First, I had to wrap my head around what I will generously refer to as his "filing system." It consisted of a whole cabinet full of unlabeled binders, each stuffed with notes. In them you could find anything from birth certificates to articles on how best to propagate daffodils. There were monthly bank statements and daily cartoons... all in random order. Basically, whenever my father wanted to keep something he'd open up a binder – any binder – and file the paper on top. The result was a mess.

Just getting the papers organized was a very time-consuming endeavor. I literally had to look at each single sheet, tossing the irrelevant and sorting the important documents into new piles. It wasn't all tedious, though. Occasionally I came across some really curious items. Dad loved talking about the past, and we had some good laughs about old stories.

And to give my dad some credit, he held on to *everything*. After all the papers were organized I could see there was nothing missing. He even had the architectural drawings for a rental property dating back to 1935!

With everything in place, the next step was to collect all the necessary data from the banks, investment firms, insurance companies, and other institutions my parents did business with. The list was long. I needed phone numbers, contact information, account numbers, addresses, and other details so I could contact them one by one to explain the situation. Most of the people I talked to knew my father personally but didn't know *me* at all. That meant that for every single transaction I had to show proof I was indeed permitted to act on my father's behalf, even though I didn't have a German residence or the proper documentation.

Over the coming months, my father's health deteriorated further. At that point my top priority was to get support for my mother, who had been caring for him tirelessly. This was when my business background started to come in handy. I was good at hiring and managing people, which turned out to be a crucial skill. We needed help. One of the first hires was an outpatient care service to support my mother with daily tasks. We also signed my father up with an adult day care center for a few days per week.

Remember this was in Germany, where health and social services are largely covered by national insurance. As it turned out, insurance paid for the outpatient care services but not the day care. Our out-of-pocket expense for adult day care came to around $70 per day, which was well worth the expense. Dad got to spend a few days each week in a safe and stimulating place while mom got a respite from the grind of being a solo caregiver.

A typical day looked like this: early in the morning the nursing staff would come to bathe and dress my father, put his compression stockings on, and inject insulin while giving him his other medications. Afterward he would be picked up and taken to the adult day care center, where he would spend the day until late afternoon. The care center provided meals and kept everyone busy with all kinds of age-appropriate activities. We were told Dad especially enjoyed the board games, even though he got caught cheating a few times.

All of these steps allowed my father to do just what he always wanted: to remain in his house until he died with no regrets two years later. He was 91 years old and had been lovingly cared for by his wife. By that time I had his binders carefully organized, with everything labeled. That made what could have been an overwhelming situation manageable. It also left me in a position to respect my mother's wishes and let her stay in the home for as long as possible, too.

I went along with her wishes, albeit somewhat reluctantly. While my mom didn't have the severe health problems my father had been enduring, she was suffering from macular degeneration. That's a condition where the patient's central field of vision is dark and the perimeter is blurry. Hers had advanced to the point that she was considered legally blind. I was worried about leaving her at home, but trusted her ophthalmologist, who remained firm in his advice not to move her unless other health issues were present. Amazingly, I discovered she was able to get around and perform most household chores while taking care of herself. Her only real limitation was that she couldn't read without a special device.

I bought the suggested reader – which Mom adorably called her "laptop" – and made some modifications to the house so it would be easier and safer for her to live in. Then, I hired more help and organized her daily care, which was very similar to my father's. After all these adjustments my mom felt safe, and most importantly content, with her stay-at-home situation.

My Mother's Weekly Routine

FOUR DAYS A WEEK she would go to adult day care. A driver would reliably pick her up in the morning and drop her off in the early evening. She would eat her meals at the day care center and could order takeout on Tuesdays and weekends using her phone's speed dial function.

TUESDAY was Mom's day off from the day care. She would visit with her volunteer companion, a woman who would spend two hours taking my mother shopping, guiding her on a walk, or just having coffee together. Not only would this amazing lady give my mother company, she would also keep track of upcoming doctors' appointments, keep an eye on food that might expire in the fridge or pantry, and forward any important correspondence to me.

SATURDAY the cleaning lady would come to tidy up the house and go grocery shopping while Mom got her hair and nails done at home.

SUNDAY was my mother's day off. The perfect time to call and catch up with her friends.

You might wonder how I was still involved. Even after the services had been put into place, caring for my mom wasn't hands-off. By the time all this was put into place, I had returned to my life and business. To manage things from afar I phoned her at least three times per week to stay up to date and deal with whatever came up. Also, the volunteer companion used WhatsApp to stay in touch with me. From paying bills and taxes to managing the maintenance of my mother's home and rental property, there were constantly things being thrown my way.

Luckily, though, because of how I had organized her life (and mine), I was able to manage just fine. And, even though my mother eventually moved to a skilled nursing facility after a fall at home, I still do today. We've managed to find a balance that works for both of us.

After her accident, my mom made me proud. There were some rough patches and a little bit of drama here and there, but all in all she handled the transition like a trouper. The day she left her house for good she simply put on her coat, grabbed her purse, and walked away. She didn't turn around and look back. Nor did she cry, which really surprised me. Looking back I'm not sure exactly what I had expected, but certainly not an attitude of "Okay, let's go."

It took me quite a while before I had the courage to ask my mom why she simply walked away from her old house in life. Do you know what her answer was? "I was longing for a new beginning."

Finding clarity in your mind about the role you want to play in your loved one's care is half the battle. For some this is easy, but others may struggle before finding the right fit.

Casting Call

What Role Do You Want to Play?

I magine for a moment that your favorite movie director was calling to cast you for one of two roles: the first is a caregiver, and the second is a care organizer. Which one would you be right for?

While some people will have no doubts in their minds about what role they can (or are able to) play in their elder's life, many will not immediately know. Most adults have not given the topic much thought at all, may be unclear about the differences, or could struggle emotionally to address their own sense of responsibility.

To help you find the right role – and possibly ease your mind – let's look at the practicalities of *caregiving* versus *care organizing*.

A caregiver, in a nutshell, is someone who provides hands-on assistance for a person who is disabled, sick, or frail. They will handle daily activities like preparing meals, administering medications, and housekeeping tasks. They might also be responsible for helping with mobility and transportation, personally supervising the elder, and supporting their physical and emotional health. The caregiver could be a volunteer, a family member, or a qualified for-hire specialist. This person should be close by and available to step in on short notice. That might sound like you. But it probably doesn't.

As noble as the intention of becoming a caregiver may seem, unless you are trained in nursing and geriatric care, you might not be qualified to provide the assistance your loved one needs. For example: a caregiver needs to be confident they can safely lift an elderly person and move them into a vehicle or away from a piece of furniture. They might have to give injections and respond quickly to medical emergencies. Would you be comfortable performing these duties?

Chances are you would not, and it wouldn't be safe for you to try, either. Depending on your cultural background or belief system, you may feel pressure to "give back" by providing care for your loved one, but that might not be the best idea for either of you. Consider how dire the consequences could be if you made just one single mistake.

There are safer ways in which you can show your gratitude toward an elder – like managing and structuring the aspects of their care – that don't necessarily require you to be physically present at all times. In other words, you could do your part by slipping into the valuable role of a care organizer. In fact, it might be the more responsible way to fulfill your obligation.

If you think caregivers are the only ones doing the heavy lifting, think twice. Your role as care organizer doesn't begin and end with hiring providers or choosing meal plans for your loved one. In fact, these actions will make up only a tiny fraction of your responsibilities. Essentially, you will be managing another person's life on top of your own. That's the part no one wants to talk about.

The profile of an organizer is a person with high personal integrity who is trustworthy and reliable. They must be honest, organized, patient, diligent, computer savvy, and good at managing people. They have to be able to wrap their heads around complex issues while remaining compassionate and empathetic, not to mention persistent and assertive. Could you bring some of these traits to the table? If so, the job is yours. But if not, you might need someone else to take on this role.

The moment you come to realize that, without your engagement, your loved one's fate would be in the hands of a stranger, you will start to grasp the significance of this job. That's when you realize becoming an organizer isn't about shrugging off your obligation to them at all. Managing care for another person is a huge responsibility.

Don't leave the decision to become a care organizer up to chance or let emotional conflicts cloud your mind. The sooner you can wrap your head around the reality that you probably aren't the best person to feed, bathe, and medicate an elderly person, the better. When you find your role, it sets the stage for everyone involved. You can communicate your plan to your elder and any other family members so there are no ambiguities. This will make it easier on everyone, and especially the person being cared for, as you move through the coming process.

There are duties that overlap between caregivers and care organizers, but I want to be clear this book is written for the person who wants to serve as an organizer.

Throughout the coming chapters I'm going to walk you through a series of tasks and methods that will help you in all aspects of organizing care for your loved one while also caring for yourself. I'm going to show you how to be organized and emotionally available for one of the biggest roles you can ever play.

Just as you would be smart to start saving for retirement early, it makes sense to prepare a strategy for the care of your aging parent as soon as possible – to handle big decisions and arrange paperwork ahead of time. The sooner you get started, the fewer surprises you'll have to deal with later.

Get Your Ducks in a Row
Organizing Two Lives

I f you're going to organize care for someone else, you should start by organizing your own life first. Why start here? There are a couple of good reasons. First, your life is something you have full control of. And second, the odds are great that you will eventually need to arrange care for your elderly parent, particularly if they are facing mental or physical difficulties in their later years. Setting the right priorities is not only important to the pursuit of your own happiness and fulfillment, but it also puts you in a better position to organize care for your loved one later, rather than making snap decisions under extreme pressure.

Managing your own time is the single most important component of your senior care plan. If you don't get a grip on your daily routine, you will constantly be stretched thin, scrambling to get anything accomplished. You can get a jump on that process now and know it will pay huge dividends later.

We tend to think of time as an infinitely renewable resource when in fact it's the one thing we need to treasure and manage most carefully. I recently came upon an article in The Harvard Business Review[1] that made this point brilliantly. Here is a brief excerpt:

Time is hard to account for – it's easily consumed, squandered, and lost. But it receives far less attention than money does. Few of us carefully budget how we'll spend our next windfall of time. We worry about wasting money on a cup of coffee every day, and how that adds up, when we should be just as concerned about all those minutes we frittered away that could have been used to make us happier. And very few of us strategize about how to gain a large chunk of time in the future, perhaps to devote to a rewarding project or to enjoy a family vacation.

*… Let's all resolve to be as deliberate about time as we are about money and work. Before spending your next cent, think about whether that purchase will enhance your use of time. Before making your next work-related decision, think about the impact it will have on your time with your family, and how much you will enjoy being with them. Remind yourself that it's not true that there will always be more time later. **There won't!***

This article really struck a chord with me, particularly as it related to the topic of planning for elder care. The odds are great you *will* eventually need to arrange care for your elderly parent, particularly if they face mental or physical difficulties in their later years. When that happens you'll need to start handling everything twice. You'll do your taxes and your parents' taxes. After paying your own household medical bills you will also have to manage (and possibly pay) your parents' medical bills, too. The list goes on and on.

Once I understood just how much time and work it took to manage someone else's life, I started carving out at least two hours per day to organize and handle those tasks. It was my way of looking after things without becoming completely overwhelmed or going insane.

If you are thinking to yourself that two hours seems like a lot of time, I would advise you to think again. Dealing with an elderly person takes far more from your schedule than you might realize, particularly

1   Time Poor and Unhappy, Harvard Business Review, January 2019

when you factor in the hours you spend dealing with administrators, bureaucrats, and third parties.

To help you understand what these two hours look like on a day-to-day basis, let me share some of the things I started taking care of for my mother:

- Correspondence
- Bill paying
- Personal income taxes
- Medical insurance
- Social Security
- Pension
- Banking
- Investments
- Real estate-related issues
- Rental property management
- Insurance issues (homeowner's, hurricane, fire, flood insurance, liability)
- Chimney sweeping and maintenance
- Heating oil orders and delivery
- Household help with gardening and housecleaning
- Doctors' visits and follow-up
- Organizing transportation
- Monitoring medical issues
- Dealing with physicians and nurses

This list could actually be longer, but you get the point. Dealing with these issues – not to mention the various people and organizations involved – is going to take time out of your day. Even if you can afford to hire help in some of these areas, you will need to manage caregivers and service providers while making key decisions and setting priorities.

To help your elderly loved one without losing your mind in the process, you have to create more hours than you had before. That's why I want you to start preparing for the inevitable now.

Setting Better Time-Management Habits

In my experience, learning to better manage time and commitments isn't just a process of absorbing information, but also breaking bad habits. I realized pretty quickly that if I was going to manage my mother's affairs, keep my business afloat, and have anything that resembled a life I would need to make some hard choices up front.

Suppose you're going to devote ten hours per week to managing the affairs of your loved one, as I do. Where is that time going to come from? It's never too late to make time a friend, rather than an enemy, and get in the habit of squeezing more out of your waking hours. Let me share a simple five-step plan that helped me free up the hours I need each week.

Let's Get Started
Prerequisites: laptop, mobile phone, scanner, printer, and internet connection.

Step 1

Work on simplifying your life by cutting back on activities and commitments that are complicating things and chewing up your time. One way to accomplish this is to simply say "no" or ask for help with chores or tasks you are normally expected to do but don't enjoy in the first place. If you have family members who aren't pulling their own weight, this might be a good opportunity to get them involved.

For example, you could ask your spouse to clean the home, have them go grocery shopping and cook, or get them to do the laundry. Maybe convince them to do *all* of these things. Perhaps your teenager could help with the garden, walk the dog, or feed the cat. You can probably find plenty of chores to delegate, although it's not always easy to recruit for these jobs.

Step 2

Stop wasting time on social media. As tempting as it may be to post the details of your ordeal to the world and get emotional support from your friends, or just see what they've been up to, it's a huge drain on your precious hours. Your time is better spent on the important tasks demanding your attention.

I installed an app called "LeechBlock" inside my web browser. It lets me choose up to six websites (in my case, Facebook, Instagram, Amazon, and a couple of others) I frequently visit. Then, I set a block of time aside for uninterrupted work. The app stops me from loading those sites while I'm supposed to be focused. It even keeps me from impulse buying shoes – *neat!*

Don't get me wrong: the internet isn't evil, and in fact many applications make it easier to manage our lives and care for our elderly loved ones. I spend a great deal of time in front of a computer for work and am always trying to use technology to my advantage. For instance, I have de-cluttered huge piles of paper documents and receipts for myself and my parents, and have streamlined various parts of my life with apps. As a result, I've freed up valuable time I can now spend on happier pursuits.

The trick is to use screen time productively... without letting it get in the way of actually living.

Step 3

Turn email notifications off on all devices and check emails only once or twice per day at a *maximum*. It would be even better to check your mail just twice per week, but not everyone can do that (I certainly can't).

Since I run a business my preferred routine is to look at new messages first at 10 AM and once more around 3 PM. My email software allows me to set alerts for VIP contacts so I won't miss time-sensitive notices. You could follow a similar system, or tweak it to match your schedule (for example, checking personal emails during lunch and again after work).

Why am I so concerned with email? It's important to eliminate as many distractions as you can if you want to manage your time effectively. Most emails simply aren't that urgent or important. Every time you stop what you're doing to open a new message you get pulled away from the task at hand. Studies have shown it can take several minutes to bring your attention back to something more important once you've been interrupted.

> "Getting better at managing my own time has probably been the most critical step in the whole process of organizing care for my parents.

Step 4

Use the Pomodoro Technique® by Francesco Cirillo for time management. The creator of this method was looking for ways to get more done in less time as a university student – and he did. He found that the human brain functions at full capacity for only around 25 minutes. Then, it needs to rest for 5 to 10 minutes before getting full effort again. What began as a simple experiment for him has now become a productivity program used by more than two million people.

To use this technique you either set a timer on your phone for 25-minute intervals or install the Pomodoro® extension on your browser. At the time of this writing there is not yet a stand-alone phone app available, but you may want to look online to see if it's available.

I have to admit I was reluctant to try this at first. Applying the technique took a bit of getting used to. Once I got the hang of it, though, I started getting big results. Now I regularly use the Pomodoro® timer for all kinds of work and personal tasks. It's like giving your brain a boost.

Step 5

Next, let's get to work and take inventory on how automated your life is. Do you ever feel like you spend too much time with banking and bills? You can keep current statements handy – and ensure you never miss another payment – by simply signing up for as many online portals as possible. Opt into autopay and electronic statements and you're good to go.

Here are a few examples of bills and chores that can be automated this way:

- Direct deposits from employers and agencies
- Everyday banking
- Investment accounts
- Credit cards
- Health insurance
- Car insurance
- Homeowner's insurance
- Rent/mortgage
- Utilities
- Internet, television, and mobile phone
- Subscriptions

None of these will be difficult to set up, and you can use a reputable password manager if you have concerns about online banking.

Getting through those five steps wasn't too hard, was it? Now that you have skimmed off a number of tasks that drain your time and energy, you should be able to treat yourself to an hour or two off. You deserve it. Remember that no one expects you to be a superhero. You shouldn't expect that from yourself, either.

Taking Care of You

How will you use the extra time carved out of your weekly schedule? I recommend you devote some of it to supporting your body, mind, and soul. Use it to improve areas of your life that are crying out for attention. Establishing a healthy lifestyle begins with taking a little bit of time for yourself – not just once in a blue moon, but *every day*.

Getting into this habit doesn't have to be complicated or expensive. In fact, the simpler you keep things, the better. As an example, daydreaming for 15 minutes when you would have been staring at a screen can do wonders for your mood. Walking around the block for 30 minutes fills your lungs, creates movement, and helps you sleep better.

This is your chance to start thinking about you. When you're feeling weary, take a nap or chat with a friend. If your marriage needs a boost, ask your special someone for date night and do some rekindling. Don't let any serious mental, physical, or substance abuse problems linger. Seek professional help and clean up any messes that require your attention.

I'm going to return to this topic again in the chapter, **Taking a Breather.** It has even more ideas on ways to create calm and strength in your life. For the moment, though, think about hopping over to YouTube for fun exercise classes if you need to lose a few pounds, or check out some tutorials on your favorite hobby or stress-relief technique. If you start taking baby steps to reach your goals and improve your life now, then you'll be better equipped to handle the workload and stress of being a care organizer later.

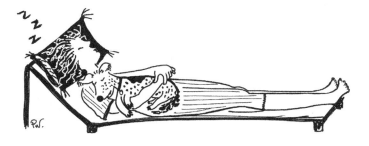

It's often little things that help to heal our minds, bodies, and souls the most. Going forward, keep asking yourself: what small changes could I make to feel better? When you find the answers, give them a try.

Depending on how well-organized you are (or aren't), you might need to roll up your sleeves for this section of the book. In this chapter we are going to organize all the important documents you need to avoid big headaches later.

All Those Pesky Documents

Life Gets a Lot Easier When You Have the Right Paperwork

I'm a pretty organized person. You have to be if you want to run your own business. When it came down to caring for my parents, though, I realized I wasn't quite as efficient as I had thought.

> *Even though I'd always wanted to go paperless, I wasn't quite there. There was a mountain of papers in my office that never seemed to get smaller – hundreds of documents begging to be scanned, sorted, digitized, and filed. It never seemed like the right time to deal with them. Or maybe it was just that I always had a good excuse ready. There was always another project or surf session calling my name.*
>
> *The tipping point came when I started traveling overseas more frequently to see my parents. I remember realizing my insurance company was canceling my policy because the autopay I had set up wasn't working. I didn't have the information I needed with me and found myself scrambling for records and account numbers while at the same time dealing with urgent issues for my parents. Everything got sorted out in the end,*

but it was a huge headache that could have been avoided. It reminded me there was a good reason for stringent record-keeping, so I made a daily habit of chipping away at that pile of papers. Progress was slow and steady, but it got shorter and shorter each week until it disappeared.

Getting myself organized was tough, but doing the same thing for my parents was downright tedious. They were born in the 1920s. Using technology to get organized was never a priority for them, so no digital files existed. Neither my mother or father knew how to operate a mobile phone or computer, and the internet was an incomprehensible entity to them.

The net result was a house with lots of really old papers and no Wi-Fi. It was time to change all of that. I set up a small workspace in their home with a desk and one of those combination printer/scanner/copier units, which proved to be an invaluable purchase. That little box saved me more hours running to the copy shop than I could count. In the end, I got all the records I needed to organize their lives and could access them whenever I needed – even from Hawaii.

If you already have your documents and affairs in order, kudos to you. If you are a meticulous organizer and have parents with automated payments and digital documents, then you are well ahead of the game.

For the other 99% of you who are just like me, here is a valuable piece of advice: don't make the same mistake I made. Not being able to locate important documents in a timely fashion could delay applications or even cause denial of certain benefits. It can lead to stress, and in some cases financial hardship, for yourself and your elder. It may also delay you from being able to travel back and forth to your loved one on short notice.

This is so important it would be almost impossible for me to say it enough – get those pesky documents in order! Rest assured that once you are finished it will give you a great measure of peace... both for yourself and those you hold dear.

Because this is so crucial, I'm going to do a couple of important things in this chapter. First, I'm going to give you a sense of which documents you need to collect. Then, I'm going to provide you with a link to some worksheets you can use to track them. Just sign up at: **theeldercareplaybook.com** to download your copy.

You'll notice the documents I provided are fillable, meaning you can enter your information right there. Or take the templates and make them your own. Only you will know what's relevant for your own unique circumstances. You can even show the blank copies to family members and loved ones to start difficult conversations or get help pulling the required details together.

Just remember that gathering paperwork is a process. There might be times when the voices in your head will say "This is too much work!" Tell them to shut up and be quiet. If you just fill in five or ten items per day, you'll have completed the job before you know it.

What Kinds of Documents Do You Need?

Here's a summary of what you will be collecting and storing into one easy-to-access place:

- Account logins
- Who's who (friends and persons of interest)
- Important records (birth certificate, marriage license, etc.)
- Financial information
- Insurance policy details
- Credit and lending statements
- Business documents
- Retirement plans & statements
- Tax returns
- Property deeds
- Equipment manuals
- Medication plans
- Wallet emergency cards
- A hospital preparedness bag and inventory

> "Verified buyers can download worksheets at: theeldercareplaybook.com Enter: MECWB to unlock.

Along with hard copies of these items, you might want to also create digital copies of important documents for quick access. You can even use a scanner or snap a photo with your smartphone to take them with you, as well as store the files on a hard drive.

Personally, I have a document with all of these files combined in one place. I store an encrypted copy of it on my hard drive so I can access it as needed while I'm on the road. The printed version (including the originals) are stored in a safe place. You might choose to keep them in a rented safety deposit box, for example, or under lock with an attorney.

If you are living in a high-crime area and can't keep these files safe without the hassle and expense of renting secure storage, you might consider bolting a fireproof safe out of sight somewhere where it's unlikely to be found (under a floor or inside a wall). You can even store another small safe under your bed or in a chest drawer – obvious places a burglar would look – and fill it with cheap items as a decoy.

Keep in mind that gathering files isn't an exercise you will only do once. I recommend you schedule a review of your master document once a year, given that some information will change over time. Keep up with that practice and you won't have to start over with a huge amount of paperwork each time.

It's also a good idea to go through the process of organizing documents twice: once for yourself and once for your parent or loved one. In addition to having the paperwork needed to manage your elder's life, you'll also want to know you can manage to travel or stay on top of your own affairs in an emergency.

You don't know me, but when I travel I start packing days (if not weeks) in advance. Most might find that highly amusing, but to me it's a crucial component of my sanity. Some might say this is the German in me, but I just know it's a habit I learned from my mother. Not only did she pack her suitcase well in advance of an upcoming trip, she also kept a packed bag containing the essentials for a hospital visit in her closet.

In the last few years, since the ordeal with my parents started, I have always kept a carry-on bag packed with the "must-haves" so I only have to throw in a few last-minute things if I'm running out the door. I'm not sure how you travel, but that's how I do it. And, I can tell you that having that bag, along with all the necessary information for myself and my mother, ready at my fingertips helped tremendously when I needed it.

Getting organized may mean keeping two sets of digital files (with each one being potentially backed up in the cloud for easy access when needed). However, there are some documents — like passports, birth certificates, and power of attorney forms — that are necessary to show as original signed or notarized copies.

You will learn through experience what you need to scan, update, or take with you when arranging things for your family member. If you are just starting out, stay on the side of caution and gather more paperwork than you think you will need into a master document with an online backup.

In case you are still not convinced that you will need to get on top of paperwork: just think of the hundreds of loose ends left behind when a loved one passes. In that circumstance every single financial institution will have to be notified, accounts will have to be closed, and contracts will have to be canceled. If you don't have the records you need, organized and accessible in a convenient place, where do you begin and who do you ask?

Very few people enjoy dealing with paperwork, but it's a crucial part of the process. Do your loved one and your future self a favor by getting your documents organized sooner rather than later.

LOGINS
last updated:

PLATFORM	USER NAME	PASSWORD	PIN CODE
Password Manager	mrsmith	dkgjur849tyg	
Password List	on computer - documents - my stuff		
Apple or Microsoft ID	myname@url.com		
Cellphone	212-612-9090	fingerprint	123456
Computer	fingerprint	mrsmith123	
iPad/Tablet			
Kindle			
Email			
Wifi			
Router Setup			
Roku/Apple TV			
Echo			
Amazon Prime			
Netflix			
Hulu			
Spotify			
Facebook			
WhatsApp			
Instagram			
Twitter			
Linked In			
Pinterest			
Shopping Sites (and others)			

DOCUMENTS & KEYS   last updated:

DOCUMENT	LOCATION	ACCESS
Wallet	*on my desk*	
Address Book	*on my computer*	
Calendar	*my leather organizer*	
Birth Certificate	*desk drawer - binder - documents*	
Social Security Card	*desk drawer - binder - documents*	
Driver's License	*in wallet*	
Organ Donor Card		
Motor Vehicle Title		
Car Registration		
Car Safety		
Car Insurance Card		
Passport		
Citizenship Papers		
Naturalization Papers		
Adoption Papers		
Marriage Certificate		
Prenuptual Agreement		
Divorce/Separation Papers		
Death Certificates		
Military Records		
Military Discharge		
Funeral /Burial Instructions		
Cemetery Plot		

DOCUMENTS & KEYS   last updated:

DOCUMENT	LOCATION	ACCESS
House & Car Keys or Opener	*in bin on console or on hook*	
Gate Combination		*#1234*
P.O. Box # & Key	*#123 - key on keychain*	
Office Key or Combination		*#1234*
Rental Property Keys	*in middle drawer of desk*	
Rental Property Combination		
Rental Agreement(s)		
Real Estate Deed(s)		
Architectural Drawings		
Appraisal(s)		
Other Title(s) of Ownership		
HUD		
Federal & State Tax Returns		
Gift Tax Returns		
Records/Receipts for Taxes		
State Property Tax Relief		
Will (Testament)/Estate Plan		
Long-term Care Plan		
Trust(s)		
Power of Attorney		
Health Care Directive		
Physician's Order (POLST)		
Do Not Resuscitate Order		

DOCUMENTS & KEYS

last updated:

DOCUMENT	LOCATION	ACCESS
Safe Deposit Box Key/Code	See Mrs. Miller @ Bank	#123456
Inventory of Valuables	in desk bottom drawer	
Location of Jewelry		
Location of Valuables		
Location of Cash		
Collectibles		

FINANCES

last updated:

	INSTITUTION	ACCOUNT-#
Checking Account	*American Savings Bank*	*#123456789*
website: *americansavings.com*	login:	*smithy gjriogr657*
contact: *Mrs. Miller*	phone:	*800-123-4561*
Savings Account		
website:	login:	
contact:	phone:	
Credit Union		
website:	login:	
contact:	phone:	
Brokerage Account		
website:	login:	
contact:	phone:	
Mutual Fund Account		
website:	login:	
contact:	phone:	
Retirement Accounts		
website:	login:	
contact:	phone:	
Other Managed Account		
website:	login:	
contact:	phone:	
Personal Trust		
Trustee Info	phone:	

FINANCES   last updated:

DOCUMENT	LOCATION / ACCESS
Complete List of Assets & Debts	*in desk bottom drawer*
Checkbook	*in desk bottom drawer*
ATM Card(s)	*in my wallet*
Online Bill Paying	*is not set up*
Online Transaction Confirmations	
Charitable Trust	
Donation Preferences	
Federal & State Tax Returns (past 3-5 years)	
Social Security Reports	
CD Statements	
Cost Basis Papers	
Stock Certs not held in an account	
Bearer Bonds not held in an account	
Alternative Investments (incl. K-1S)	
529 College Savings Plan Statements	
Concentrated Stocks (10b5-1 Selling Plans, Rule144/145 Sales and Lending)	

You might want to include a list of routine household bills and records of any personal loans made to others and where you keep them.

Information on bank contacts, financial planner and tax accountant can be found under the section *"Who's Who."* Designating beneficiaries and listing them for every bank account or investments should not be forgotten, it removes the hurdle of going through probate.

FINANCES

last updated:

ACCOUNT	BENEFICIARIES	CONTACT	AS OF DATE
Checking Account	1. Ben Smith	bensmith@gmail.com	1/1/1990
	2. Gina Gold	ggold@yahoo.com	1/1/1990
Savings Account	1.		
	2.		
Brokerage Account	1.		
	2.		
Mutual Funds Account	1.		
	2.		
Retirement Accounts	1.		
	2.		
Managed Accounts	1.		
	2.		
Other Managed Accounts	1.		
	2.		

RETIREMENT   last updated:

	INFO	USER/PASSWORD	STATEMENTS
Social Security	*111-22-3333*	*bensmith*	*$eirt3891 socialsecurity.gov*
Pension Plan	*General Motors HR, Mr. Williams, ph: 800-816-4321*		
Traditional IRA			
Roth IRA			
SEP IRA			
Retirement Plan(s) from All Employers e.g. 401(k), 403(b)			
1. Employer			
2. Employer			
3. Employer			
4. Employer			
Stock Options			
Deferred Compensation			
Royalties			
Variable or Fixed Annuity Statements			
Beneficiary Forms for IRAs, 401(k)s or Other Benefit Plans			
Beneficiary Forms for Annuities			
Life Insurance Benefits			
Waiting Lists/Contracts with Retirement Communities			
Waiting Lists/Contracts with Nursing Home			

INSURANCES

last updated:

	INSTITUTION	ACCOUNT-#
Medical Insurance	*Kaiser Permanente*	*#981643*
website: *kp.org*	login:	*smithy gjriogrb51*
contact: *Mrs. Jones*	phone:	*800-321-6154*
Dental Insurance		
website:	login:	
contact:	phone:	
Medicare Number & ID Card		
website:	login:	
contact:	phone:	
Medicare Savings Program		
website:	login:	
contact:	phone:	
Medicare Prescription Drug Coverage		
website:	login:	
contact:	phone:	
Secondary Medical Insurance		
website:	login:	
contact:	phone:	
Medicaid Number & ID Card		
website:	login:	
contact:	phone:	

INSURANCES

last updated:

	INSTITUTION	ACCOUNT-#
Accident Insurance	AIG	#4563182
website:	aig.com	login: smithy gjriogr657
contact:	Mr. Sullivan	phone: 800-561-2345
Vehicle Insurance		
website:		login:
contact:		phone:
Disability Insurance		
website:		login:
contact:		phone:
Long-term Care Insurance		
website:		login:
contact:		phone:
Life Insurance		
website:		login:
contact:		phone:
Group Life Policies		
website:		login:
contact:		phone:
Mortgage Insurance		
website:		login:
contact:		phone:

INSURANCES   last updated:

	INSTITUTION	ACCOUNT-#
Home Owners Insurance	*State Farm Insurance*	*#123456789*
website: *statefarm.com*	login:	*smithy gjriogrb57*
contact: *Mrs. Howard*	phone:	*888-323-8567*
Personal Property Insurance		
website:	login:	
contact:	phone:	
Casualty Insurance		
website:	login:	
contact:	phone:	
Liability Insurance		
website:	login:	
contact:	phone:	
Veterans Administration Insurance		
website:	login:	
contact:	phone:	
Travel Insurance		
website:	login:	
contact:	phone:	
Beneficiary Forms for Policies		
website:	login:	
contact:	phone:	

All Insurance Bills are kept in:

CREDIT & LENDING   last updated:

	PORTAL	USER/PASSWORD	PIN
CC American Express	americanexpress.com	smithy bnnkfH#mje4394	
CC Visa Card	citi.com	wanda kfl;hsgkdhsg748	
CC Master Card			
CC Citibank			
CC Diners Club			
Shopping Cards			
Frequent Flyer CCs			
Gasoline Card			
Other Credit Cards			
Mortgage Lender			
Mortgage Papers			
Mortgage Bills			
Home Equity Loan			
Loan Mgmt. Account			
Statements			
Online Transaction Confirmations			
Securities-based Loan			
Car Loan			
College Debt			
Promissory Notes			
Other Outstanding Loans			

BUSINESS

	LOCATION	ACCESS
Incorporation Papers	n/a	
Ownership Papers	n/a	
Business Registration	n/a	
Financing Papers		
Bank Account		
website:		login:
contact:		phone:
Investment Account		
website:		login:
contact:		phone:
Business Loan		
website:		login:
contact:		phone:
Payroll Records		
Employee Records		
Health Insurance		
website:		login:
contact:		phone:
Employee Retirement Plans		
website:		login:
contact:		phone:
401(k) Matching		

BUSINESS   last updated:

	LOCATION	ACCESS
Stock Option Plans *n/a*		
website:		login:
contact:		phone:
Pension Plans		
website:		login:
contact:		phone:
Other Employee Benefit Plans		
Buy/Sell Partnership Agreements		
American Express CC		
website:		login:
contact:		phone:
Visa Card CC		
website:		login:
contact:		phone:
Master Card CC		
website:		login:
contact:		phone:
Citibank CC		
website:		login:
contact:		phone:

BUSINESS   last updated:

	LOCATION	ACCESS
Diners Club CC *n/a*		
website:	login:	
contact:	phone:	
Other Credit Cards		
Employee Credit Cards		
website:	login:	
contact:	phone:	
Business Contracts		
Rental Contract for Business		
Employee Contracts		
Attorney		
Deeds for Business Property		
Corporate Tax Accountant		
Corporate Tax Accountant		
Sales Tax Records		
GE-Tax Records		
941-Filing & Reporting		
940-Filing & Reporting		
State Withholding Filing & Reporting		
SUI Filing & Reporting		
W2s / W3s		
1099s		
Other Tax Forms & Filings		

PROPERTY MANUAL

last updated:

DETAILS
Emergency Contact/ Security *Mr. Johnson; 201-981-5613*
Property Manager *Mr. Brown; 201-981-5614*
Plumber *Roto Rooter; 800-888-4444*
Electrician etc.
Gardening
Garage
Garbage Service
Turn on Water Main
Fuse Box
Utility Meter
Septic Tank
Cesspool
Chimney
Propane Gas
Heating Oil
Air Conditioning
Thermostats
Washer
Dryer
Freezer
Refrigerator
Stove / Oven
Small Appliances

WHO IS WHO   last updated:

	NAME & CONTACT
Family Team Leader (if any)	Ben Smith bensmith@gmail.com 314-456-148
Backup Person	Gina Gold ggold@yahoo.com 916-841-6935
Closest Friend 1	Molly McDonald 212-633-7190
Closest Friend 2	
Closest Friend 3	
Distant Relative 1	
Distant Relative 2	
Distant Relative 3	
Neighbor 1	
Neighbor 2	
Neighbor 3	
Landlord	
Primary Care Physician	
Dentist / Hygienist	
OBGYN	
Ophthalmologist	
Surgeon	
Other Physician	
Home Health Aide	
Physical Therapist	
Massage Therapist	
Hair Stylist	
Pedicurist	

WHO IS WHO   last updated:

	NAME & CONTACT
Who does finances and pays bills?	*Ben Smith*
Who maintains living situation?	*Ben Smith*
Financial Advisor / Planner	*Charles Schwab, Mr. Bolton, 212-600-1111*
Accountant	
Attorney	
Executor	
Guardian for Elder or for Minor	
Agent Holding Power of Attorney	
Trusted Contact	
Telephone Provider	
Cellphone Provider	
Phone Bill Low-Income Assistance	
Cable/Satellite Provider	
Internet Service Provider (ISP)	
Gas / Power Company	
Low Income Home Energy Assistance (LIHEAP)	
Veterinarian	
Pets' Age, Feeding & Medication	
Petsitter	
Plan for Pet Care	
Church & Community Memberships	
Real Estate Agent	
Driving Service (Transportation Assistance)	

MILESTONES

DATE	WHAT HAPPENED
2/14/1952	got married
8/6/1954	bought Pontiac
3/8/1955	Ben was born

MEDICAL HISTORY   last updated:

DATE	MEDICAL ISSUE	PHYSICIAN	TREATMENT	RESOLVED
5/1952	broke shoulder	Dr. Bill	cast and rehab	yes
4/1961	hernia	Dr. Cool	surgery	yes

CURRENT MEDICATION   last updated:

NAME OF PHARMACY	PHONE #	ADDRESS
Costco Pharmacy	212-896-5882	

NAME OF DRUG	DOSE	WHEN	HOW	WHY	PRESCRIBER
Prinivil	10mg	once	with meal	hypertension	Dr. Moses
Flonase	spray	onset		allergies	Dr. Moses

PAST MEDICATION & ALLERGIES   last updated:

NAME OF DRUG	CONDITION TREATED	WHY DISCONTINUED

ALLERGIC REACTION	MEDICATION, FOOD OR OTHER SUBSTANCES	TREATMENT
Grass, Pollen	Mushrooms, Mint	Flonase

IN CASE OF AN EMERGENCY   last updated:

NAME	Michael Smith
DATE OF BIRTH	12/2/1932
ADDRESS	
PHONE	
1. EMERGENCY CONTACT	
2. EMERGENCY CONTACT	
PHYSICIAN CONTACT	
INSURANCE	
MEMBER #	
HEALTH CARE DIRECTIVE	
ORGAN DONOR	

IN CASE OF AN EMERGENCY

MY MEDICAL CONDITION	Hypertension
MY ALLERGIES	
MEDICATION	

We all age, but we don't necessarily do it in the same way. Before you jump to any conclusions or prioritize specific steps, you need to assess the health status and living circumstances of your elderly loved one.

Watch and See

Assessing the Situation

N ow that you have created an organizational masterpiece, it is
time to look at your loved one's situation. Can they manage their
life on their own or are they in desperate need of assistance? You don't
need to wait for an accident or devastating diagnosis to start thinking
about what you can do to help. In fact, I would encourage you to find
out what they can (or cannot) do independently the next time you visit
and take note of it.

Aging is a process. We are all getting older from the first day we
are born. However, just because someone has *aged* does not necessarily mean they have to move into a long-term care facility. I have met
90-year-olds who feel younger and more active than others do at age
50. Some researchers even tell us that 90 is the new 50.

The point is that we all age, but some of us handle it better than others. The challenge for you is to understand what type of assistance your
elder needs and figuring out when the time is right to transition your
aging loved one toward comprehensive assistance and care.

Since this isn't always a straightforward call, except in cases where a debilitating illness or injury forces your hand, I want you to assess their health status and living circumstances as objectively as possible. So, before you charge ahead and draw any conclusions about whether or not your family member is already a candidate for assisted living or a nursing home, trust your eyes instead of your assumptions.

The first issue to assess is your elder's driving ability.

Don't Hit the Road, Jack

When we see an older person shuffling along, hunched over, and climbing behind the wheel of a car, we freak out. Even though it is not a pretty picture, it is not a reason to panic, just something that needs to get addressed.

From the outside, we all know it's not safe. And yet, it's nearly impossible to reason with an elderly person and convince them to give up their license. It might be disturbing for the rest of us, but they don't want to give up their independence, so they hang on to their automobiles as if their lives depended on it. To do so would mean losing the ability to get around without assistance, and to impose their transportation needs on friends or family members.

If you want to keep your senior (and the people around them) safe, you have to come up with a plan to either make driving work or find alternatives. This could involve engaging volunteers and looking into municipal services. It might also mean overcoming your loved one's arguments to help them get around safely. AAA has a website devoted to this topic, which can be found at **seniordriving.aaa.com.** It's a great resource, and even shows how you can jumpstart the difficult conversation of convincing your loved one to give up their driver's license.

As you explore your options, remember that driving isn't just about hitting the open road. For seniors, transportation problems can often hinder self-care and medical treatment. You might not want your loved one driving around, but you don't want them to be cut off from the world (and especially grocery stores, medical providers, etc.) either.

Watching Closely

Driving issues might be obvious to the naked eye, but other problems or changes might require closer observation. Look closely and you may notice your senior is not as capable as they once were. How concerned should you be?

There is no particular need to worry when your loved one performs certain tasks at a much slower pace than you're used to seeing – that is simply part of the aging process. While a gradual change in someone's capabilities might require some assistance on occasion, rapid behavioral health changes could indicate the need for a swifter response.

Physical issues tend to be easier to observe than cognitive difficulties. It's hard to know what's going on in someone else's mind, and senior adults can be good at hiding their struggles from others (particularly their children). That's why you'll want to interact with them on a daily basis to establish a baseline and get a true sense of how well they are or aren't getting along on their own.

When you are around your loved one often, the changes can be subtle. Infrequent visits can lead to bigger shocks. For example, you might have the sense from a distance that Mom is doing fine. When you see her yourself, though, you may notice her legs are feeble and she isn't able to get up from her favorite chair without struggling. She could be less active because she's feeling a bit doddery and weak. Perhaps that's why the kitchen is a mess, the pantry is half-empty, and her once-tidy household appears to be neglected. These are all signs an elder isn't managing that well and might need some assistance.

In general, you'll want to pay attention to how well your loved one is managing in the areas that make independence possible:

- Mobility
- Cognitive and communication skills
- Self-care
- Planning day-to-day activities
- Maintaining social contacts

- Keeping an orderly home
- Using things we take for granted (like technology)
- Any obvious signs of physical or psychological deterioration

By looking at your loved one's day-to-day life in this way, you can get a better understanding of the situation both of you are facing. That can help you determine whether you need to act, and how soon. Later in the book I will share some ideas on making their home environment safer. For now, just observe and take notes.

Also keep in mind that no one likes to be analyzed. Be discreet through this process. Just watch and see during your interactions how tasks are being performed. You can make notes later. There are going to be some routines you can't observe, such as using the bathroom or taking a shower. If you can talk openly with your loved one about these issues, that's great and you should do so. If not, consider posing your questions indirectly. For example, you might say something like: "My friend's mom was always wobbly on her feet when using the shower. Her daughter recently got a special chair for the bathroom and it made such a big difference for her. Let me know if you need one and I can ask her where she got it."

Your Assessment Checklist

You can use the following brief checklist to evaluate how well your senior can manage the activities of daily living, as well as their general well-being and safety.

I am using numbers 1-3 to measure level of difficulty, with one indicating the person is able to perform a task without problems, two the person is having some difficulty and three the person's ability is severely impaired and not able to perform the task without any help.

MOBILITY

How independently can the person move and change the position of his or her body? Is moving around at home possible?

Walking: stable and with steady gait? Or unstable?

(While shuffling is normal at a certain age, it suggests a propensity for falls. See chapter section **Home Smarts** *for fixes)*

Uses correctly measured walking aid properly

Climbing and walking down stairs

Getting in and out of chair

Getting in and out of bed

Getting in and out of car

Needs to be laid in bed

Needs to be turned in bed

Needs body mobilization

Shows signs of a recent fall

COGNITIVE AND COMMUNICATION SKILLS

How is the person's orientation in relation to time and place? Can the person make decisions for herself or himself? Can the person hold a conversation and communicate his or her needs?

Reading

Listening

Comprehending

Articulating

Driving a car

Using public transportation

Leaving the house

Finding the way home (has gotten lost)

Recognizing friends and family

Communicating needs clearly

SELF-CARE

How independently can the person care for herself or himself in relation to personal hygiene, eating and drinking, or getting dressed and undressed?

Eating

Drinking

Consuming beverages throughout the day

Getting dressed or undressed

Using the bathroom (pulling down/up pants, cleaning up)

Washing hands

Brushing teeth/flossing

Cleaning dentures

Shaving

Washing/combing hair

Skin care

Nail care

Taking a shower or bath

Using and maintaining hearing aid

Using and maintaining glasses

COPING AND DEALING INDEPENDENTLY WITH ILLNESS AND TREATMENT-RELATED DEMANDS AND STRESSES

What kind of assistance does the person need to deal with his or her illnesses and treatments? How often is assistance necessary for taking medication, changing wound dressings, or seeing doctors?

Keeping medication in a safe place

Taking medications as directed

Putting on or taking off prosthetics

Self-administering oxygen, injections, or wound care

Emptying a stoma pouch

Hooking up a feeding tube

Giving insulin injections

Putting on or taking off compression stockings

Weight management (obviously gaining or losing weight)

PLANNING DAY-TO-DAY-LIVING AND MAINTAINING SOCIAL CONTACT

How independently can the person still arrange and plan their daily schedule? Can they maintain social contact?

Keeping a calendar

Retrieving and reading the newspaper

Phoning a friend or family member

Going to or participating in social activities

Initiating conversation with the neighbor

KEEPING AN ORDERLY HOME

Cleaning/maintaining a home (keeping things reasonably clean and tidy)

Gardening

Doing laundry

Ironing/folding laundry

Putting laundry away

Making the bed

Changing bedsheets

Grocery shopping

Going to the mall

Prepping food and snacks

Cooking meals

Doing dishes

Keeping an orderly, well-stocked pantry

Keeping cleaning supplies at hand

Keeping refrigerator clean (is food rotten or expired?)

Picking up and emptying trash bins

Disposing of incontinence articles

Heating/cooling the home

Pulling up and lowering blinds

Turning lights on and off

Checking mail

Caring for pets adequately

Emptying and cleaning toilet pan

USING THE THINGS WE TAKE FOR GRANTED (TECHNOLOGY)

Is the person able to utilize everyday tools and conveniences?

Driving safely

Using the TV remote control

Using telephone or mobile phone

Putting batteries in hearing aid

Using stove/oven/microwave

Using washer/dryer

BEHAVIOR AND PSYCHOLOGICAL ISSUES

How often does the person need assistance because of psychological issues (e.g., aggressive or anxious behavior)? Are they doing harm to themselves or others? Are they overly trusting of strangers, or mistrusting family members?

Aggression

Paranoia

Wandering

Cognitive changes

Panic disorder

Anxiety disorder

Obsessive-compulsive disorder

Depression

Delirium

Trouble adjusting to life changes or medication

Shows signs of side effects of medications

Anger/outbursts

Stressors can lead to depression and anxiety. Common stressors include grief, poverty, medical challenges, functional limitations, chronic pain, and struggling with the burden of care for an infirm family member. Identifying, and if possible removing a stressor can make a big difference.

> "You will want to have a baseline you can refer back to when contemplating your next step, both now and in the future.

Making Sense of This Checklist

The purpose of this checklist isn't to arrive at a definitive score or decision. Instead, it's to help you think about the struggles your senior may be facing so you can either help to arrange care or enjoy the peace of mind that comes with knowing they can manage on their own.

Some capabilities and daily chores are more critical to a person's well-being than others. With that in mind, here are a few telltale signs a situation may not be safe:

- The person cannot get in or out of bed without assistance.
- The person cannot use facilities alone.
- The person cannot walk or falls frequently.
- The person cannot articulate their wants or needs.
- The person cannot use the bathroom independently.
- The person misses medications.
- The person misses meals.
- There is a lack of personal hygiene.
- The person is disoriented or sleep walks.
- The person leaves the door unlocked.
- The person leaves stoves on repeatedly.

Behavioral or psychological changes are especially difficult to pinpoint and deal with. You could evaluate an elderly person on one day and feel as if they are mentally clear and competent only to have someone else tell you they've been talking utter nonsense shortly thereafter. Your senior could become paranoid. They might start giving money away, or dating "the love of their life" without warning. They might claim that someone – maybe even you – is stealing from them or abusing them. It can be difficult to evaluate or argue with these bizarre behaviors, so what are you supposed to do? Your first step is to get to the bottom of any conflicting information. Find out whether the stories are real or imagined. Then you can protect yourself, reassure your elderly loved one, and take the proper next steps.

Once you have added your scores together and examined the list of red flags above, write down the resulting figures and today's date. This becomes your baseline you can use to compare to future checks at regular intervals.

SCORED **1** _____ TIMES

SCORED **2** _____ TIMES

SCORED **3** _____ TIMES

In your assessment, where is help needed the most?

_____

LAST UPDATED: _____ (*insert date*)

After you've completed your assessment checklist, compare your findings to the impressions of others – particularly those who might be closer to the situation. These might include neighbors, close friends, or health care providers who can give a different perspective. Just remember that some of the people you asked for feedback might exaggerate, or even lie, for their own reasons.

Aging can be a slow process, or it can move very quickly. Circumstances can change in the blink of an eye. Keep that in mind and note any changes in your senior's condition whenever possible. It is almost inevitable that, at some point or another, an older adult will become increasingly helpless. Or their lives may change instantly when an unexpected event – like a fall or sudden illness – leads to immobility, cognitive decline, or some combination of both. The assessment list can come in handy under any circumstance when you want to compare a "before" and "after."

So When Do You Have to Spring into Action?

To recap, a significant proportion of older people experience dependency for the first time in the later stages of their lives, often as a consequence of age-related decreases in functional capacity. As they lose hearing and vision, or deal with the progression of disease, they might not be able to do some of the things they used to do. How do you know when to step in?

Just because a senior has slowed down, don't necessarily assume that means their whole life needs to be turned upside down, or that there is a need to hire a full-time in-home care professional. Making the home safer to avoid falls, for instance, while hiring someone to help with the heavy lifting in the household might do the trick and preserve their independence. They might not need help with most daily activities. By leaving things for them to do, you can help them maintain their place and keep their spirit alive.

Up until a few years ago my mother was still taking public transportation, fetching her groceries, cooking her meals, doing her laundry, and generally keeping her household in order. She was dealing with severe vision impairment. Yes, she looked like your typical old lady. Her linens weren't perfectly pressed anymore, and her floors were less than sparkling clean. But she properly kept her household, and in truth probably did more than I would on a normal day. It was only when her gait became unstable and she needed to use a walker that she realized the days when she would zip up and down the stairs or hop on a bus were over. One day she admitted it would be nice to have someone do the laundry and clean the house for her. Finally!

My mother might have looked and acted her age, but she wasn't ready for a nursing home yet. She still found purpose in maintaining her household. As long as I felt she was safe in that house I didn't see a reason to make her move. So, I gladly arranged for help in the areas where she needed it most.

Your loved one may follow a similar path, or one that is very different. The time to intervene is when you have answered most questions in the survey between levels 2 and 3. At that point it's clear the person can no longer function independently, and may pose a danger to themselves or others. That's when you should explore possible caregiving arrangements.

Conversely, if the majority of your answers have landed on level 1, and only a few on level 2, then it may be the case that the person isn't able to perform certain functions but is largely independent. They may even be capable of arranging their own help or assistance by doing things like calling a cab or ordering takeout food. In that situation, simply monitoring the situation with regard to mobility, self-care, and cognitive changes (noting any signs of deterioration) could be the best way forward.

Before you come to an answer, let me share two important pieces of advice.

1. Don't Rush*

Some late-life problems can result in depression and anxiety. These include physical health challenges, the responsibility of caring for a spouse with dementia or physical disability, managing conflict with family members, and especially grieving the death of loved ones.

Getting the appropriate treatment for these mental conditions early can make a huge difference in an older person's well-being. Sadly, the elderly often end up in nursing homes shortly after their spouses pass

---

*Unless a medical emergency warrants immediate action

because they are depressed and anxious, suddenly finding themselves at home alone for the first time in many years. Instead of giving them time to properly grieve and adjust their lives to new circumstances, they are yanked out of their comfort zones. That's a double whammy that should be avoided whenever possible. Allow your loved one time to grieve and show them lots of empathy.

> Observe your elderly parent, listen carefully to others, and trust your gut feeling.

2. Consider Your Own Situation

Do you have the skills required to care for your elder? Are you constantly flying across the country to deal with new emergencies? Is the financial strain of caring for them too much for you to shoulder, or is the situation wreaking havoc on your family life, relationships, or career?

Be honest with yourself. Are you having trouble sleeping? Are your friends worried about you? Do you feel anxious all the time? These are all indications you're running out of steam. While the focus of this chapter is on evaluating the health and safety of your loved one, it's worth remembering that you need to look after your own well-being at the same time.

The question of when it's time for your loved one to change their living arrangement, arrange for in-home care, or perhaps even move into a nursing home is one only you can find the answer to. I hope I have given you the tools you need to make the right assessment and decision.

After you have assessed the situation it's time to start a dialogue. You will want to understand your loved one's vision of how they wish to live their remaining years and how they are planning to pay for it.

Having the Talk

Speak Your Mind and Make a Plan

In an ideal world, we would all be having proactive discussions around aging scenarios while our parents are still relatively young. We would get together, talk about their needs, and construct care plans while they are healthy and fit. Unfortunately, you and your family members probably feel uncomfortable bringing these issues to light – just like most people – and will wait until a turn of events makes it impossible to ignore them any longer.

Most seniors aren't going to put detailed wishes down on paper, which usually means relatives will have to rely on their own recollections and impressions. They may find themselves scrambling to divvy up responsibilities when disaster strikes. This is common, but it isn't inevitable. Aging is an essential part of life's progression; why not prepare for our later years while we still have the capacity to do so? My guess is that it's because none of us has a crystal ball. We can't imagine the bad things that could happen to us, and certainly don't want to spend too much time thinking about them.

Putting things off doesn't solve the problem, though. For the potential care organizer, it's extremely important to get answers to pressing questions early on. You need to know what really matters to the person you love, what their values are, and (especially) how they wish to spend the rest of their lives. When you're equipped with that information, you can prepare ahead of time and reach consensus with family members on who will be in charge of carrying out these wishes if there isn't an obvious candidate.

What if you were to get ahead of the problem and bring up elder living or care choices today, before crisis strikes? What if you were able to get a general idea of your parents' wishes for what could happen when they become fragile, are unable to perform daily activities, or (worst case) cannot make decisions on their own? What if your loved ones told you how they want to spend the time they have left? By working together with them, and other family members, you could come up with workable ideas and establish roles. You could figure out what you are able to handle and which parts of the process you don't want to be in charge of. These conversations might be difficult, but they can benefit everyone.

As an example, let's say your loved one is still fairly active and would rather have fewer chores while residing among people in a similar age group. They might not know how to accomplish this, but with a bit of research you can help them settle into an *independent senior living home*.

Or, let's imagine your family member wants a particular friend to be involved in their care if they become ill. However, you've never even heard of this friend. It's time for you to collect the details and get to know this individual so you can make arrangements.

Maybe your parent is adamant about aging in place until the very end and there is no way – under any circumstances – they will change their mind. You need to know that so you can prepare the home for age-appropriate living accommodations, and potentially hire outpatient care services as needed.

Make no mistake: your life will be impacted no matter which decisions or preferences your senior has. Having the information about their wishes will help you immensely in understanding what might lie ahead and how you can plan for it.

Over the course of several years, Dad and I more or less joked about the topic of "an old fart's existence." We discussed how hard it would be to give up driving the car, and whether it would be more difficult to turn in his keys or let Mom change his diapers. I came away from these conversations with a fairly good understanding of my parents' vision for their future, but the picture was still a bit muddled. It was heavy on theory and light on practical ideas.

> Having "the talk" can be eye-opening and a big relief. It's not something to be afraid of.

Because I had experienced a sudden turn of events with my brother's passing, I knew well that it could happen again. My organized self was seeking a roadmap, and it wanted it sooner rather than later. I felt acutely aware of the fact that I was the only one left who could step in to make decisions on my parents' behalf if needed.

When Dad started to slow down, the topic became a much heavier one. We had to stare an uncomfortable reality in the face. I wanted concrete answers so I could stop agonizing over how he would be cared for and let go of my worry about what would happen to my mother when he passed.

One day we were sharing a cup of coffee, our favorite pastime. I decided to get the answers I needed. I started off by saying I wanted to find out more about my parents' vision for the future, and their wishes, so I could fulfill them when the day came. I told Mom and Dad I didn't want to wait for another crisis to strike, or to have to make decisions for them in an emergency. I let them know I'd rather be able to discuss their wishes ahead of time while they could still express them clearly. In addition, I reminded them it takes time to get the right plans in place – especially given that we lived so far apart. If we weren't prepared, something could happen that would lead to an undesirable outcome for all of us, and my parents in particular.

Initially, Dad made an attempt to be funny and avoid the subject.

He jokingly told me my parents would simply turn all their problems over to me without any worries or stress, and that I could move in and take care of them. He was obviously dwelling in nostalgia, suggesting that as a young and healthy person I would have limitless availability to pitch in. They wanted to put all their hopes for longevity on my shoulders, or so he said. I think Dad was testing me and holding on to a slight glimmer of hope that I might agree.

"Seriously, Dad? That's not going to happen... or do you really think Mom wants me to change your diapers?" I was trying to keep the conversation light while at the same time masking the fact I was afraid I would appear unhelpful, unkind, or unloving. To say "no" seemed really harsh at the moment. I didn't want to burst Dad's bubble, but I knew it was absolutely necessary to be honest and make myself clear. Dad knew very well, of course, that our lack of proximity and my work situation made his scenario rather unrealistic. He was aware they would have to lower their expectations. I just hoped he wouldn't hold it against me that my hands were tied and there was only so much I could realistically do.

Beginning that conversation was difficult, but once the initial awkwardness was out of the way we could FINALLY get serious and begin discussing possible solutions.

What I learned was this: both my parents wanted to remain in their house, taking care of each other, for as long as possible. With my help they would hire skilled nursing staff, along with other support when Mom needed a break. Once that became too burdensome, they agreed to either hire an in-home nurse or move into a nursing facility.

Fair enough. It sounded like a good plan – at least for the moment.

As it turned out, I later discovered this roadmap was nowhere near as complete as it could have been. I came to realize we didn't have a thorough enough understanding of all the different care options available to us. The plans we created mostly came from observing what others did. In the end, those impressions didn't mean squat when it came time to follow through.

It's one thing to state "I am staying put" and another to do it successfully as we age. It took a lot of time and research, running around and interviewing various service providers, and trial and error along the way to get things right.

Even though no one can predict the future, you need to open up dialogue while your aging loved one can still share and express their wishes. It's the only way you'll be able to later honor those wishes for someone you care so much about.

Engaging Other Family Members

Are there others in your family who will be responsible for looking after your loved one, or making decisions that will impact their care? It's time to get them involved.

Creating a comfortable environment where everyone in your family can speak freely and be heard isn't always easy, but it's important. Otherwise you might never get the answers you seek. When there are multiple siblings involved, and possibly stronger or weaker members in the group, using a democratic vote or vote by committee to bring everyone to the table can be the most sensible route. Instead of having the strongest voice assume decision-making on behalf of the rest the family, everyone gets to have an equal say so you can reach a real consensus.

You don't need permission from your aging parent to start this discussion, but you should inform them about your plans before the committee sits down to have "the talk." Reassure your elder that the family members have agreed to a process to create structure, keep everyone informed, and ensure nothing is being hidden from the senior. Let them know they will always be kept in the loop if they wish to be. Remind them that the group has only one interest, and will approach every decision with one question: "What is the right thing for our loved one?" Everything else should be set aside.

The first step is to gather all the family members together. Ideally this would happen in person, but you could meet on a conference or video call. Begin by deciding who will become the group's speaker. The spokesperson's responsibility is to take notes, schedule meetings to keep everyone informed, and execute decisions. This person should also remind the group regularly that, above all, the goal is to do what is best for the senior. The ideal candidate for this role is someone who is "neutral," with a calm disposition, a trustworthy demeanor, and the heart of a diplomat to negotiate positive outcomes.

The spokesperson privy over anyone else. All members of the committee have equal rights and say. You can literally vote on any topic, but should keep voting anonymous to avoid any bad blood. The group has to understand that during an emergency there may not be enough time to call a committee vote – especially if members are in different time zones or aren't always reachable – but typically everyone should be involved so everyone is comfortable and can trust the process.

How democratic do you need to be? That depends on your family dynamics. Keep in mind that it's only natural for each member to have their own agenda and motives. In some cases those might not always align with what is in the best interest of the elder.

No matter how transparent the process, there may be conflict or disagreements. To see why, let's look at an example of a situation where decision by committee may create additional obstacles. In our hypothetical example there are three siblings. One is financially strapped, the second is emotionally codependent on the elder, and the third has no obvious baggage. The sibling with no baggage may seem like the obvious choice for the job of spokesperson, but in reality he or she may be judgmental and envious of "special treatments" the weaker links in the family have received over the years. Things suddenly aren't as clear or easy, are they? In a situation like this it may be advisable for the parent to assign an independent party he or she can trust, and one that isn't tied to money or favors. Families can be pretty screwed up, and the more members there are the more drama and obstacles you have to overcome.

Once you have those logistics and family dynamics squared away, it's time to tap into your elder's mind…

Let's Start Talking!

Before you dive straight into having "the talk" you need to be clear in your own mind about what answers you are looking for so you can be sure all of your concerns are being addressed. If you are afraid you will have a hard time keeping your thoughts organized while talking, write down your questions in advance. You could also ask a friend to practice with you beforehand. This could be a difficult and emotionally charged conversation. A little preparation can go a long way.

Below are examples of things you might want to ask. Personalize this list by considering your own circumstances and adding the questions that matter the most to you.

Here are some good questions to get you started:

- What are your wishes if you become very sick and are unable to speak for yourself?
- Do you have an estate plan, health care proxy, and long-term care plan?
- Where would you live if you needed care?
- What would you do if you became more fragile and needed care?
- Who would take care of you if you needed assistance?
- How would you organize care for yourself?
- What would prompt you to move out of your home?
- How would you pay for it?
- What kind of medical treatment would you want me to reject or agree to?
- Have you given durable power of attorney to anyone?
- If you became mentally or physically disabled, what would be most important to you?

Did you notice how these questions put your senior in charge of their future?

Once you have your script in place, aim for an opportune moment to bring up the subject. Timing is everything! Make sure neither of you is tired, in pain, or emotionally stressed. You'll want everyone to be relaxed and in a good mood.

If you're not sure how to start the conversation, consider mentioning this book. You might say: "I just finished reading this book on organizing care for an aging loved one. After reading it, I started to wonder whether I really know what your wishes are in the event that you need to be taken care of in the future. Would you please share with me what your wishes are, and what preparations you have made?"

Chances are you won't get answers to all of your questions in one sitting. Even worse, you might not get *any* answers at all the first time you ask. Don't worry, just keep at it. Addressing these topics is a process and speaking about future plans will get easier with time. Your ultimate goal is to come away with a game plan, of course, but for now all you really have to do is listen and take in what your loved one has to say.

During your conversation(s) you might learn that your loved one has already prepared an estate plan or long-term care strategy. If so, that's great! Ask if you can review the plans together and make sure you fully understand the details. If, on the other hand, no preparations have been made, then encourage your senior to consider starting soon. Let them know you'll offer a helping hand. Don't forget to follow up in a timely manner – it's not easy to get this process started, and it would be unfortunate if momentum was lost.

Along the same lines, you might discover that your loved one's estate plan does not directly spell out long-term care options. It might be that your senior created it many years ago and wasn't thinking that far ahead. Or, they may have been confused about available care options (as so many people are). The situation isn't uncommon, and it can be fixed. I'm going to address that topic in more depth later in the book.

Don't be surprised if family members have contrasting views when it comes to where an aging adult ought to reside for the remaining years of their life journey. Try not to get emotional about it. Remain calm and speak in a supportive way. Don't put anyone on the spot, and don't point out all the things your senior can't do for themselves. They are very aware of their own limitations. Keep your focus on gathering information. Your parent may have an outdated perception of assisted living facilities or nursing homes. They might not know

> Give your parent a voice and have them take ownership of the outcome early on.

how modern residential care has changed, or which potential benefits could be included. Just knowing they don't have all the facts gives you valuable insight into their thinking.

This is a good point to mention again that as long as your parent is managing fairly well, you should try to help them preserve their independence (assuming that's what they want). You could suggest hiring household help, bringing in a handyman for home maintenance, or signing them up for dependable services that deliver meals, pay bills, provide transportation, or offer personal care services. If finances are an issue, know that many communities have aging and disability resource centers to assist in finding low-cost providers or volunteer services. If your loved one is hesitant to accept the cost, remind them that they deserve to have the things they need to make life easier for themselves. Your goal is to slowly decrease their responsibilities while increasing in-home safety and ensuring they have access to good physical care. Every little bit of help you add over time makes a difference.

> *My mom was never into sports or games but she had an active social life. She loved to bake and cook, attended her garden, and kept up with all the entertainment news. Shortly before she turned 90 she told me her brain felt more like that of a 78-year-old woman's, but that she wished her aching joints felt as young as her mind. I realized then that, when the day came, she would need to be in a mentally stimulating environment. Mom had to be in a place where social engagement was going to be encouraged.*

Look for opportunities for social connections to prevent isolation. As comfy as their home might be, encourage your aging parent to get out of the house as often as possible. When older adults remain at home alone, they inevitably become more and more isolated. Loneliness and social isolation, in turn, have been linked to poor health outcomes in seniors according to a study by researcher Nicholas R. Nicholson and "A Review of Social Isolation," published in *The Journal of Primary Prevention*[2].

If they are reluctant to get out, keep in mind that by addressing hearing and vision impairments, incontinence issues, or a poor body image you can help your loved one connect with – and remain connected to – others without embarrassment.

Making the Case for a Move into an Appropriate Care Facility

Ideally, your loved one will continue to be in good enough shape to

2   Nicholas R. Nicholson, "A Review of Social Isolation," *The Journal of Primary Prevention*, 2012, 33 (2-3): 137-52 http://www.aidschicago.org/resources/content/1/0/8/9/documents/04-reviewsocisolationnicholson.pdf.

age in their home for many years. But what happens if, based on the evaluations you've been making, it becomes clear your senior needs high-level, round-the-clock care? You'll have to grab the bull by the horns and make the argument for a move into a place where they can receive the help they need. If you are uncertain of what type of facility is right for them, I cover the big choices (and how they differ) in the chapter titled **Know Your Options**.

Discussing this might leave you feeling uneasy, and you may not be sure how to gently raise the subject with your senior. Your inclination might even be to avoid addressing the topic altogether. That's understandable, but there isn't any way to escape the truth. If the time has come, don't wait – sit down and have a heart-to-heart talk about the situation. Speak your mind clearly. If you have multiple family members to consult, voice your concerns and state firmly that it's time to talk about transitioning your elder into an appropriate care facility. Present your plan to the group and let everyone be heard. Then, make suggestions on living options based on the knowledge and research you already put together.

> The most important consideration is always safety before comfort.

There is a good chance you will experience some pushback. Your loved one may fear losing their personal dignity, freedom, and control. Let them know you understand how scary it must be to leave behind familiar surroundings, and share your own worries. Tell them you also hold these fears and that you'll do everything in your power to not only find the right place for them, but to ensure they are well taken care of. Let them know they'll be treated with love and compassion. As long as you show you are sensitive to your senior's feelings and show them you will have their back, they'll feel validated and respected. Most of all, make sure your elder understands that even though the expense of their ailments is having to move out of a comfortable home, it doesn't necessarily mean that they won't ever be comfortable and content again. They will always be loved.

Make the person who will be receiving the care the leader of your discussion and have them contribute as best they can when it comes to planning for such a move. Allow them to contemplate and share any scenarios that might come to mind, regardless of how realistic they seem. By acknowledging the move as a chance to shape the future instead of having a stranger make decisions for them, you can give your aging parent power over their own destiny. In that way you can gently guide them along to ensure a positive outcome. Everyone benefits when the focus is put squarely on purposeful living.

Without making false promises, you should discuss with them a step-by-step plan on how the move and transition into new living quarters will go forward. The more detailed your plan, the better picture you can paint and the easier it will be for your loved one to warm to the thought of moving. Keep in mind that some assisted living homes even allow applicants to "test drive" the facility for a period of time, usually as long as two weeks. Also remember that a move doesn't have to be made all at once; transitioning in small steps toward a larger change gives everyone a chance to adapt comfortably and feels less dramatic. Take advantage of those options.

Once I figured out how to improve my mother's surroundings and organize her daily living activities, things were going pretty smoothly for both of us. To many, myself included, it was astounding how well she managed on her own. But suddenly all of that changed.

Last year an unfortunate fall brought everything I had so carefully assembled crashing down. The moment Mom "kissed the floor" she knew that was it, and that I would not let her continue living alone in her house. Neither of us brought up the dreaded "NH word," perhaps feeling as if we could prevent the inevitable if we didn't mention it out loud. Instead, my mother began apologizing for her fall and searching for a way to undo the accident.

She pleaded with me indirectly: "Can't I just continue the way I have for a little bit longer?"

"Let me ask you this, Mom," I answered. "What went through your head when you fell and tried to get back on your feet? How did you feel?

There was no one there to help you up and you forgot to press the emergency button, right?"

There was a long pause. She responded: "I had panische Angst," which is German for "I was petrified." Then she continued. "It was awful. I wouldn't want to experience this again… In a nursing home this couldn't happen, right?"

"Mom, falls can happen anywhere. Even in a nursing home. But there you would get skilled help. The nurses know exactly what to do and can respond to an emergency the right way."

It was my mother's "angst" that acquainted her with the thought of moving out of her house. Of course, I would have preferred she never had such an experience in the first place, but prior to that fall I couldn't bring myself to force her out. It just didn't seem right.

Helping Your Loved One Make a Difficult Decision

In case you lack persuasive arguments for nursing home living, here are a few ideas you can use to jumpstart the dialogue:

- The loss of long-term control when no decision is being made. For example, after hospitalization, a doctor might write an order for your loved one to be moved into a facility that is not one of your choosing. Ask: *"Wouldn't you rather pick your own than lose your freedom of choice?"*

- One of the most powerful and persuasive realizations is that a patient might be assigned to share a room in a nursing facility that is been chosen by doctors because they cannot be sent home due to safety concerns. Ask: *"Do you really want to share a room, and a bathroom, with another person you don't know?"*

- Another good one: *"Once you're placed in a nursing home it is very difficult to change if you don't like it. It takes time and money, and another move would be extremely stressful for everyone involved. If we start looking now and find one you like, we can put your name on the waiting list."*

- On the subject of waiting lists, it only makes sense to point out that with a quickly growing elder population, most good nursing facilities have long waiting lists. If you or your loved one has their eyes set on one in particular it's best to get your name on that list as soon as possible.

- Here is another thing to consider: you, as the care organizer, may not be present when something bad happens to your aging parent or loved one. Then, you may be forced to make a less-than-ideal decision from afar, which could result in a bad situation that is difficult to change later on. Ask: *"Wouldn't you rather have me to shop around with you while I'm here?"* Note that by "shopping" you really *do* mean shopping because that's all you'd really be doing in the beginning stages.

If your parent doesn't want to hear any of these arguments, or is completely uncooperative, you might be in for a rough ride. Heart-wrenching decisions might have to be made. If that's the case, read on.

Rarely are all ideas and perspectives going to be in sync. Unfortunately, this too often leads to family disputes and unnecessary frustration. It's sad, but many families are split apart by senior care decisions because they cannot come to an agreement that works for everyone. At a time when love and compassion should rule, our egos and priorities clash.

Why is that? Don't we all want the same thing – comfort and security?

The reason why our goals might not quite align with those of our loved ones is that we are trying too hard to accommodate opposite sets of needs. Your need, as a care organizer, is to quickly fix the situation and get on with your own life. Yet the person who needs to be taken care of would rather maintain the status quo even though it comes at the expense of their own well-being (and possibly yours, as well). Change is particularly frightening when you are older, and seniors often feel backed into a corner when they are being sold on the idea of moving out of their homes.

How Can We Find a Common Denominator?

My best piece of advice is to do what I advised earlier and ask what *exactly* your parent or loved one is afraid of. Give them permission to articulate their worries and acknowledge their fears: of losing control, losing their spirit, being put into a corner, or maybe even worries about being abused. *Simply hear them.*

Many older adults cannot imagine life in new surroundings and are afraid they will have to get rid of most of their accumulated belongings. They might fear having to say goodbye to their well-worn sofa. They can worry about uprooting their life for an unknown future, or being alone in an unfamiliar place. The list of fears, both rational and irrational, is almost endless. There is only one thing you can do to help, and that is acknowledging how hard it is to let go.

> Hold their hands, give them a big hug, and give these concerns the validity they deserve.

Tell your loved one you understand these concerns and feelings. Don't just say it once; *tell them over and over again.* Let them know you are making the decision to move them with a heavy heart, but with the best intentions toward a positive outcome. Reassure your parent you will do everything in your power to allow them to have a voice throughout the entire process, and that you won't ever leave them to become a victim in an abusive situation. Your senior might just need that extra reassurance that you are looking out for them, and that you want their comfort and security just as much as they do.

After showing your empathy for their worries, make sure you are heard, too. You might be hesitant, but you should also share your own thoughts respectfully. You might say something like: "*I don't want to complain, but this really weighs on me. For months I haven't been able to sleep at night because I constantly worry about you. My job has suffered because I'm not fully present. I really wish we could find a long-term solution. Of course I will not force you to move into a nursing home against your wishes, but please consider the consequences of staying put. Are you sure that's what you want?*"

By showing how their decisions affect your life, you are making them accountable for their actions and inactions.

Another crucial part of this conversation is discussing your own personal and financial situation. Don't shy away from expressing how difficult it could be for you to maintain your career over the course of many years of caregiving. Now is the perfect time to weigh in on possible future scenarios so your loved one understands the issues you're facing and can tailor their expectations.

Remember the elderly want to be assured they will be well cared for while knowing that their children and loved ones will be okay, too. Once your family member sees how your life is being affected by an untenable situation, they might be more open to considering a change in living arrangements.

Is It Time to Talk?

No one can predict the future. That's why you need to open up a dialogue with your aging senior while they can still clearly express and share their wishes. It's the only way you will be able to honor those wishes later.

The purpose of having this kind of conversation early on is to discover what the elder has on his or her mind, and what their vision for the future looks like. It's not for anything else. When you're equipped with that information, and your assessment of the actual situation at present, you're one step closer to figuring out what will come next. That might be something as little as making a mental note of their wishes and concerns.

Unless there is already a clear indication your loved one needs high-level 24/7 care, this is not the time to pressure your elderly family member into doing something they aren't comfortable with. Show empathy for their worries and communicate clearly that you will put your best efforts forward, while being mindful of your own boundaries and limitations, when it comes to organizing their future care.

Allowing someone to take a close look into, and ultimately manage, your financial and medical affairs isn't easy. When you look into your elder's life it might feel as if you're opening the drawer to someone's underwear – it's uncomfortable for them and you don't necessarily know what you'll find. Who wants to dig through Granny's balbriggans? And who wants another person picking through their g-strings?

Trust Me

Handing Over the Reins

Reasonable people understand why it's important and necessary to appoint someone they trust to handle their money and affairs if they can't do it themselves. It's entirely logical for an aging person to do this when they are *able* in case they later become *unable* to do so.

Reasonable people can also bring several people together to a table to discuss how they plan to hand over the reins in the future. And, reasonable people will do this at a time when everyone is relaxed and comfortable, rather than being forced into action by an unforeseen emergency. Finally, reasonable people will see why having a lawyer set up a durable power of attorney (DPOA), an essential document when someone can no longer take care of his or her affairs, is a crucial step toward planning for the inevitable. To get an elderly par-

> However, in some families reason or logic is not often applied.

ent to agree to even *discuss* their finances – let alone think about giving up control – is a huge deal for most. It is, however, also the most important topic people purposefully ignore or dismiss until it's too late.

What Is Power of Attorney (POA)?

According to Wikipedia, a power of attorney (also known as a POA or letter of attorney) is a written authorization to represent or act on another person's behalf in private affairs, business, or some other legal matter. The person authorizing the other to act is the *principal, grantor, or donor* (of the power). The person authorized to act is the *agent, attorney* or, in some legal jurisdictions, the *attorney-in-fact.*

There are various forms of POA depending on how much power you want to grant someone. However, the only one that's relevant in situations where mental or physical impairments become a problem is the *durable financial power of attorney* (DPOA). It allows the agent to make **all** decisions on personal or business affairs on behalf of the grantor. This is the only power of attorney document that *doesn't* terminate when we become physically or mentally incapacitated, the time when it is most critical. It is also the one and only document to open doors to health information or any other records for the appointed agent without any hassle – a critical consideration when governments change data protection laws.

The DPOA can be *immediate* or *springing.* Springing means it requires one or two physicians' statements of incapacity to activate. However, those declarations are becoming increasingly difficult to obtain under modern privacy laws, so it may be preferable to have your senior make a DPOA immediate and name someone they fully trust as an agent.

A DPOA terminates on death, which means the grantor will have to name the same agent (or a different one) as the executor in his or her will, or as successor trustee of the trust if the grantor wants the agent to continue on after they have passed.

It is a common misconception that a senior needs a power of attorney only *after* they lack legal capacity to manage their own affairs. However, if and when aging prevents them from making sound decisions and they cannot manage their finances any longer, it is already too late to set up a DPOA. At that point the person would be deemed unfit to enter into a legally binding agreement, meaning they would not have the legal capacity to sign off on such a document. In that situation the only way for someone to act on their behalf is by court order through a guardianship or conservatorship. These kinds of court proceedings can take a long time and may prevent the agent from acting on important matters (such as signing a contract to the nursing home of the parent's choice).

At one point my father presented me with a handwritten "power of attorney" and insisted that, because it was signed by him and witnessed by my mother, it was a legally binding document. He was convinced he did the right thing – after all, he had started his working career as an apprentice for an attorney. As it turned out, he was mistaken. It was painful to watch his face when I told him the piece of paper had become useless because of changes to German law. And it was rather frustrating that there was no changing his mind when I wanted to have the documents set up properly by an attorney.

The rude awakening came when his bank wouldn't grant me access to his account using his version of a power of attorney document. He had holdings that were rapidly losing value; you could literally watch years of savings going down the drain overnight (Dad wasn't a savvy investor, but that's another story). Somehow we had to figure out a way to get into the account and act.

Unfortunately, at this point Dad wasn't in good enough shape to go to the bank and talk to them in person, so I arranged a house visit. On the day of the meeting, Dad was in good spirits and made light conversation with the bank representative. Eventually she asked: "Will you give your daughter power of attorney over your account?" There was a long stretch of silence. "Sir?" Still no response.

Finally, with a chuckle Dad said: "Sure, she can take my money and spend it all. She can do with it whatever she wants, maybe go on a cruise. She has my full permission." Mom and I both cringed, and laughed awkwardly. This was so not the appropriate answer. What the representative didn't know was that it'd been a long-standing joke in our family that when my father was no longer around we would splurge. As expected, however, the bank associate didn't find any humor in it.

When it was time to leave, the bank agent turned to me at the door and said: "Your father has dementia and is legally unfit to make sound decisions. You will need to present something from a lawyer before we can make any changes. Good luck with that."

I stood in the doorframe afraid I would cry – I was so upset. I wasn't sure what was worse, admitting that my father's mental fitness was declining so rapidly or knowing that some stranger was holding his lifetime of savings (or whatever was left of it) hostage. My poor mother was equally shaken up. The only one who wasn't troubled was Dad, because he didn't quite understand what had just happened. I had a lot of explaining to do.

At the wee hour I dragged both my parents to an attorney and had her create durable power of attorney and health care directive documents for both my parents. This was most likely possible because I was the only remaining child. In more complex situations it probably wouldn't have been so straightforward.

In the end we dodged a major catastrophe. But it was close.

> Get this important fact across to your loved one so they can process it as soon as possible.

It cannot be stressed enough that the time for your senior to give durable power of attorney to someone they trust is *while they are still legally competent.*

There is a reason most seniors are extremely hesitant to enter into a DPOA: with that document in place, they literally give their agent access and power to *everything* as long as they are alive. That includes the power to buy or sell investments, the power to buy or sell real estate, and even the power to put an elder into a closed institution against their will. You name it, the agent can do it.

It's understandable that a person might be skeptical of such a document. And, it explains why seniors need to be very careful about who they select as agents.

We all know family dynamics can be tricky, and offspring may not always be the ones best suited for taking on this *huge* responsibility. Sibling rivalries, both old and new, can get stirred up during the process. In many cases it might be better to avoid them altogether. With that in mind, let's remember that an *agent* does not have to be a *family member.* It can also be someone unrelated to the senior. The most important thing is that it's a person with great integrity who is savvy enough to understand the responsibilities. It should be someone the elder knows will act in their best interest, will avoid conflicts of interest, and will keep good records. It should be someone they can trust to keep their property and belongings separately from the grantor's. The senior needs to have **100% TRUST** in this person.

Actually preparing a DPOA, living will, and advanced health care directive won't take long and is a relatively inexpensive process. The small effort and expense required are well worth it, given that it can avoid court proceedings for a spouse, child, or partner when a senior becomes incapacitated.

Help your elderly loved one put matters into perspective. Remind them they are not handing over the crown jewels, just making it easier for the person they appoint to act in their stead... and even then, only if the situation calls for it. Help them help themselves by loosening the grip on their affairs.

One more detail to consider: even though the DPOA is considered a legally binding document that is widely known and recognized, there are some banks or brokerage firms that

> The last thing your loved one wants is for important matters to fall into the hands of a judge or a detested relative.

will want you to use their forms. It's best to check with the institutions your loved one does business with, and to fill out and sign any necessary paperwork they provide in front of a notary public. Some states require you to execute documents in front of a witness. In addition, if a senior gives you authority to handle real estate transactions, a copy must be filed with the local lands record office. For these kinds of complex transactions be sure to check out your state's requirements, as they vary from one to the next.

While you can find a ton of advice and information online, as well as legal planning forms that are easy to download, you should always consult a lawyer for advice on your own unique circumstances. An online form can't cover all scenarios and state laws, and it's important to get the details right.

Can a senior change their mind about giving someone else power of attorney? Absolutely. One thing every older adult and care organizer should know is that the grantor can revoke or change a DPOA agreement at any time so long as they haven't been deemed incompetent.

> "The DPOA is the one document you really don't want to mess up.

That's a good thing, right? It makes sense for the principal, but it isn't always good news for the agent. Consider this: suppose your parent is approaching the time when they will need someone to act on their behalf. However, imagine they chickened out and reverse the agreement just before that happens. Where does that leave either of you?

This kind of thing happens more often than you might think, probably because we worry about losing power over our own lives as we age. So, we change our minds before we lose our minds.

With this unfortunate possibility looming, you might want to include protective provisions in some documents to safeguard against last-minute changes in times of diminished capacity. These details can help you protect yourself and your senior when it counts.

And if your elderly loved one refuses outright to give up control of their finances and affairs? Do your best to learn where important documents and records are kept so you can find them if and when they are needed. That's all you can do for now, other than hoping for a better conversation in the future.

It's time to find out whether your loved one has a long-term care plan, and if they do, what kinds of details it contains. Knowing that everything has been prepared and clear instructions are in place can give you peace of mind and take away ambiguity.

The Long-Term Care Plan
Why Everyone Needs One

We all want to be able to make our own decisions for as long as possible, and to maintain control over our own lives. But, when the day comes when your senior can no longer care for themselves and needs to rely on someone else to act on their behalf, they will want to be sure they have chosen the right person who will respect their wishes. They will want to know that their vision for care and lifestyle is understood and respected before they hand over the reins.

The best way for your elder to express their thoughts is through a long-term care plan (also called the caregiving plan). In many cases, this document might be part of a bigger estate plan. But either way, there are a number of benefits to having written guidelines in place. Not only will it minimize the kind of last-minute scrambling and family arguments that commonly arise when decisions about care are being made, but it can also help reduce the financial strain on everyone involved.

Getting into the complex details of estate planning and long-term care strategies is beyond the scope of this book. However, what I do want to make crystal clear is that you absolutely should find out whether or not your loved one has a plan in the first place. Do you know whether your parent has a plan, and who has been chosen to make decisions for them if and when they can't speak for themselves?

This paperwork should go beyond a simple will that assigns ownership of property when your parent dies. The kinds of plans I'm referring to are prepared by elder care attorneys and will spell out instructions that are to be followed when the senior doesn't have the capacity to make choices or express their preferences. They should specify how long they would want to be kept alive, and what measures they would want medical providers to take or not take.

Having the right documents is also a smart way to prepare for the future and protect family assets against expensive assisted-living or nursing home costs, not to mention preserving eligibility for Medicare assistance. Contrary to popular belief, these topics aren't only concerns for elderly people, retired individuals, or the wealthy. Anyone who owns a car, furniture, or the other trappings of modern life can use one. It doesn't matter whether they are married or single, or if they have children or don't.

It's important to know not just whether a plan is in place, but also what type of documentation has been prepared. Then you can move into the details and content. For instance, your parent may have a living trust, an irrevocable trust, and/or a will, along with an estate tax plan or long-term care plan to help outline their wishes and protect financial assets. It's also crucially important to have an advance health care directive or living will, as well as a durable power of attorney.

You will want to know about these details before you assume control of care for your aging parent or start managing their finances. Because this is such a big and necessary step, it's worth examining a few scenarios you might run into.

Scenario: A Plan Exists

If your loved one has any of the aforementioned plans in place, you'll want to know where you can find them, how you can access those documents, and when they were last updated. As a rule of thumb, any estate plans, wills, etc., should be reviewed and updated at least every three years.

After locating the documents, carefully review and discuss the details with your parents so that you have a clear understanding of your role. Make sure you know how you will be expected to execute their wishes. Also think through the practical and financial implications. Ask your loved one how they intend to finance long-term care. If there is a trust, ask if it has been fully funded.

A good next step would be to determine when and how your loved one's representative – which could be you or someone else – will take on the authority to act. Usually this would be accomplished by the person's voluntary written resignation, or by obtaining one or more "declarations of incapacity" from your senior's physician. You will need to read the necessary documents, and possibly consult with an attorney, to make this determination.

In most cases, long-term care plans will be discussed with all parties involved before they are finalized. And of course, this is the ideal solution. However, it does happen that these kinds of documents can be created in a vacuum, or without outside consultation. When that occurs, it may or may not be possible to modify the documents depending on your parent's capacity and the legal guidelines in your state.

Assuming the documents have been set up professionally, and with the best of intentions, the responsibilities placed on the person providing or organizing care should be practicable, rational, and fair. If you discover that unreasonable demands are being imposed on you, however, speak up and discuss the matter right away so that you can find a workable middle ground.

In the same way, if you've been named as a caregiver or care organizer and know without a doubt that you will not be able to take on that role, or are simply unwilling to do so, make it clear that someone else needs to be appointed. When discussing the content of a long-term care plan, it's best to leave behind any feuds, ill feelings, and lingering resentments among family members in order to achieve a consensus.

Should you be up against those emotions, or you're facing communication barriers, focus on the ultimate goal of getting the right care and assistance for your elder in the future.

Scenario: No Plan Exists

Even if no thought has been given to making arrangements for unfortunate events like disability or mental incapacity, it might not be too late to nudge your loved one into preparation. In fact, it might not even necessarily be a bad thing that they don't have anything in place – yet.

Your loved one might actually be grateful that you're starting the conversation and seek your guidance. They might have even thought about creating plans themselves but felt stressed about dealing with complicated matters. Or, they could be dealing with declining health or thinking through an upcoming medical procedure and didn't know where to begin making preparations. Either way, this could be your chance to have them get the professionally prepared documents they need.

Regardless of how that initial conversation goes, once the topic is on the table you should urge your loved one to contemplate their wishes for future care. You may also want to have them consult with an elder care lawyer, as well as a tax accountant, even if they are still relatively young and healthy. Getting advice from a reputable attorney who specializes in estate planning might also be advisable, particularly if real estate, business succession, or other complicated family issues are involved.

Note that a lot of professionals specializing in elder care can address several of these issues all at once, including:

> *Bringing up these topics isn't that easy for an aging adult and can weigh on their minds.*

- General estate planning
- Planning for incapacity with alternative decision-making documents

- Planning for possible long-term care needs, including nursing home care
- Locating the right care and coordinating financial resources to pay for it
- Ensuring the client's right to quality care

To get a general idea and find out more about estate planning, visit **estateplanning.com/What-is-Estate-Planning**.

As always, you'll want to help your senior find the right professional to work with. Have them ask lots of questions before hiring someone or paying a retainer. Here are a few tips that might help:

- Think ahead about the issues you'll need help with so you can find a relevant expert within a specific legal practice.
- Search the nearby area and identify at least three possible candidates.
- Interview any attorneys you plan to hire, and do it in person if possible.
- Make sure you understand the details, like terms and payments, before you make an agreement.

To find a specialized attorney in your area you could visit The National Academy of Elder Law Attorneys, Inc. (NAELA) online. Their website has a useful "attorney finder" feature at **https://www.naela.org/findlawyer**.

You could also ask someone you trust. In fact, many accountants, bankers, and other professionals would be happy to recommend a professional from their network.

> To find out more about estate planning visit estateplanning .com/What-is-Estate-Planning.

Questions to Ask an Attorney or Elder Care Lawyer

- Does the lawyer speak your language?
- Does the lawyer practice within your state and specialize in the areas you're planning for?
- Does the lawyer practice international law (if applicable)?
- Is the lawyer willing to meet with you for an initial consultation, either free of charge or for a fee?
- Can the lawyer show proof of experience with similar cases? Ask: "Would you please describe your experience in [insert specialty] matters?"
- Does the lawyer have a good reputation?
- Do the lawyer's credentials check out? For instance, have you entered their name and bar number into the Bar Association website for your state?
- Has the lawyer been publicly disciplined?
- Has the lawyer explained topics and made sure that you and your loved one understand all relevant issues?
- Is the lawyer's staff professional? Did they return your call promptly?
- Is the lawyer available to take your case within the timeframe you want it resolved?

Remember that you don't have to choose the first lawyer you meet. In fact, it's reasonable to shop around for the right legal representation.

Before meeting with potential attorneys and asking questions, your senior should summarize their situation, along with their needs, and write down some notes they can bring to the meeting. That way, the case presented to each attorney will be consistent, making it easier for you to compare responses later.

Also keep in mind that an experienced elder law attorney may want to meet with your loved one alone so they can assess their capacity and ensure they are not being wrongfully influenced. Your senior needs to be able to make independent and logical decisions, so don't be offended if they ask you to step away for part of the consultation.

Once your parent or loved one has decided which attorney to work with, encourage them to make a complete plan, and address the following issues dealing with retirement, disability, or death:

- Naming a caregiver or care organizer
- Distribution of assets
- Transferring or closing a business
- Planning to minimize taxes, court costs, and legal fees
- Disability insurance to replace income
- Long-term care insurance to pay for nursing homes or other expenses
- Selling property to pay for care
- Life insurance to provide for family upon death
- Naming an inheritance manager
- Naming a guardian for minor children
- Instructions for care in case of disability
- Instructions for passing on valuables
- Providing for special needs family members (without disturbing government benefits)
- Considering family members who need protection from creditors
- Considering family members going through divorce
- Passing on values about religion, work ethic, education, etc.

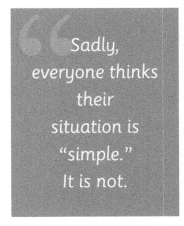

Sadly, everyone thinks their situation is "simple." It is not.

Of course, if mental competency is an issue, it may not be possible to create essential documents. In that event, court proceedings to obtain authority over your loved one's physical and/or financial affairs may be needed.

Scenario: Person Displays Irrational Behavior

In the unfortunate event that your senior shows irrational responses when you ask about estate planning and long-term care, try to evaluate the situation. Are they simply being stubborn and having a senior moment, or are they showing real signs of paranoia? It's understandable that your loved one might worry about people stealing from them, or feel trepidation about the thought of someone else making decisions for them. That's different from the kind of mental decline that would make them unable to sign legal documents or commit to future plans.

If there is real doubt, a trip to a geriatric care specialist for evaluation might help. It could be the first step in getting your aging parent on a treatment plan – or, in a worse situation – having the courts involved.

It's always better to have an estate plan in place when a person is deemed to be incapable of caring for themselves. However, if that's not possible, consultation with an attorney will be necessary because you will likely need to go to court to obtain the authority to assist your loved one going forward.

Advance Health Care Directive

As part of your loved one's caregiving and estate plan, they should have an advance health care directive (AHCD) and Physician's Order regarding Life-Sustaining Treatment (POLST).

The AHCD can be completed and signed with an attorney. The POLST is a directive for first responders who need to know your senior's resuscitation wishes. It can only be completed with the assistance of that person's physician (not an attorney). Burial and funeral arrangements might also be included in the document depending on your state, but most do not include these instructions.

Warning: Look Before You Leap

One of the most common mistakes made in the long-term care planning process is giving away real estate or other assets without consulting an attorney first. This happens frequently, especially when seniors or their family members are in stressful situations.

There are complex laws governing such transfers that can have significant tax consequences or keep families from receiving government assistance when they need it. Don't try to handle these kinds of transactions or transfers alone. Get help from an experienced attorney who can guide you.

Being Prepared for Long-Term Care

When a person becomes incapacitated, having an up-to-date long-term care plan in place can help preserve assets and make things easier for everyone involved. It will also help your senior trust the people they have put in place to assist them.

If your aging parent is resistant to creating and examining their important documents, you might remind them that without the right paperwork, state law will direct their choices and the distribution of their assets. That may or may not align with their wishes. In the same way, a public court proceeding could be needed in order for a loved one to assist in managing personal and financial affairs. Not only is that process very expensive and time-consuming, but it is also open to the public. That means anyone, even your nosy neighbor, could get a close and personal look into details of the estate.

Your loved one's estate plan and long-term care plan consist of important and ever-changing documents. These should be reviewed every three years at a minimum – and possibly more often whenever circumstances change within the family (e.g., divorce, the birth of a new grandchild, financial distress).

Even without these kinds of life changes, plans should be revisited regularly. What's on someone's mind today can be very different tomorrow. Additionally, laws and financial details change all the time and can affect a senior's plans in unintended and unforeseen ways.

Does your aging parent or loved one have a plan, and do you know how to access it? Have you read the documents that have been prepared, and do you fully understand them? If not, now is the time to talk with your senior, as well as any relevant attorneys or advisors.

And, while we're on the topic, have you given any thought to preparing an estate and care plan for yourself? If not, when are you going to do it? Remember, aging is not the only reason people become disabled or need assistance. You need to look after the senior in your life, but if you want to do yourself and your family a favor, you will take care of your own affairs, too.

At some point you will have to open the vault and dig deep into the personal and financial affairs of your loved one. After close examination of bank statements and relevant documents you will have a better understanding of whether your parent can afford care, and how much.

Skeletons in the Closet

The Things You Didn't Know

E ven when you have been granted a durable power of attorney, and have been assigned to act as a health care representative, things might not get easier. In fact, you might find yourself in a precarious situation – a place you really didn't want to be. That's because you may suddenly be confronted with family secrets or uncomfortable facts. Could it be that the precious "crown jewels" your parents were holding on to look more like plastic beads? Is it possible there was an affair that led to a sibling you didn't know about? Oh, the things you didn't know…

When I was given permission to access Dad's highly guarded "secrets" I was really nervous. It felt really awkward, as I was going through his stuff. What would I find? A weird "snooping" sensation overcame me even though I didn't just have his permission but was expected to look through his things.

Luckily, there were only a few small surprises and not anything that would have jeopardized my parents' future well-being. My father might not have been the smartest when it came to managing his assets, but all in all he took care of his wife and family. To my great relief there wasn't anything that couldn't be fixed... and more importantly, there weren't any other children or wives coming out of the woodwork.

From gambling addictions, love letters stashed from a secret affair, or hidden treasures, people hide a lot of things from each other. It happens even in the best families. So, I want you to be prepared for the fact you could stumble upon an unexpected skeleton or two in your loved one's closet. Handle whatever you find tactfully and with respect for the person who granted you the permission to look into their innermost secrets.

> Your loved one has the personal and legal right to privacy.

Remember any issues that need to be addressed should be discussed calmly, and without judgment or confrontation. Tempting as it might be, refrain from sharp criticism, mockery, or most importantly gossip. No one has the right to know about deeply personal matters except the agent, unless that person has explicitly permitted you to share the information with a third party. Your loved one has the right to keep private things confidential and be treated in a dignified manner, regardless of how juicy their story might be. It is not your job to judge or abuse the power you were entrusted with. Your job is to make sure that the elder is being taken care of, nothing more.

Furthermore, the role of an agent comes with legal restraints that could land you in trouble if you violate them. As an agent you have a strict fiduciary duty to act in the best interests of your loved one, and not your own.

What if you find out, for instance, that your parent has stashed away a small fortune despite always keeping you on a short lease? Put bluntly, it's none of your business. Your feelings don't matter, neither does your own financial situation. You might feel tempted to siphon off a little here and there for personal gain. Not only does that violate your loved one's trust, but it's also illegal. As an agent for the person in your care you are accountable for everything you do on their behalf.

You might find an unexpected treasure or embarrassing secret. Either way, act as ethically and professionally as you would want someone who was dealing with your affairs.

Good preparation starts with being educated about available care services and living options, as well as how they differ in serving the individual needs of an aging adult. Many questions need answers.

Know Your Options

Deciphering Living Options and Senior Care Services

D eciding when the time has come for your loved one to move into a senior living facility can be nerve-racking. When is it too soon and when is it too late?

Most adult care professionals will advocate for an earlier transition rather than a later one. Their argument is that it's easier for a mentally and physically fit adult to adjust to a new environment and get to know new people. Putting aside the major consideration of cost for a moment, this makes sense. If you imagine a living environment that caters to, and attracts, equally active seniors and then adjusts to their needs as age-related issues take hold, then your senior should theoretically want to move long before they need to.

In practice, however, things don't work that way. In my experience there are very few mentally and physically fit adults found in senior home settings. And I have yet to meet the person who willingly decides to spend the rest of their life in a nursing home. Instead, the majority of residents in these facilities are there because they suffered some form of health setback or handicap that made it impossible for them to live in their familiar surroundings.

As if the timing of a move to assisted living weren't a big enough challenge to consider, anyone looking into options will be confronted with a booming market filled with confusing choices. Just Google "best senior living community" and see what comes up in your results. Many will be retirement communities for those age 55 and over. That's not what I would be looking for, at least not for my frail parents. Dig deeper and you'll find a number of different housing distinctions: senior, independent, assisted living, continuing care retirement communities... the list goes on and on. Would you intuitively know which one is right? Probably not.

I've heard it said many times that it's hard to find good home health services and living facilities for seniors. I couldn't agree more. Even though there are many to choose from, it's difficult to know which one is right. Have you ever found yourself staring at a grocery store aisle, overwhelmed by too many products to choose from? That's how it feels when you're confronted with the myriad of business models and marketing pitches related to senior care. On paper, many of the living concepts appear highly promising. But at the end of the day, none of them can guarantee your loved one's well-being and happiness.

> More about this topic at seniorliving.org/life

The only thing you can do is thoroughly research the options and keep an open and creative mind. Bundle that preparation with a bit of luck and I would be surprised if you couldn't find a great place for your senior to stay.

In this chapter, I want to give you a broad overview of the housing possibilities that are available for the aging, and to teach you about various senior care services. This is certainly not a complete guide to senior living, but instead my attempt to shed some light on the various options that exist for you and your elderly loved one. In a later chapter I will go into more detail about how to actually choose and pay for the right ones.

While you read the descriptions to come, I want you to consider a few things: if you and your elder were to choose one of these options, how would he or she be cared for? Would housing and care be integrated? How involved would you need to be? Keep in mind your goal as a care organizer is not to do more, but less.

Let's start by looking at the housing choices for older adults:

- In-home care/mobile nursing service
- Adult day care/respite care
- Senior living apartments
- Independent living senior apartments
- Assisted living apartments
- Naturally occurring retirement community (NORC)
- Continuing care retirement community (CCRC)
- Board and care homes/adult foster home/personal care homes
- Skilled nursing care homes
- Memory care
- Palliative/hospice care

Living Options and Services

One term you will find in all the literature describing senior living options is *activities of daily living* (or *ADL* for short). At the most basic level, these are defined as bathing, dressing, and personal care – all the things we normally do on a daily basis. It is important to pay attention to what extent these services are being provided, as well as whether they are scheduled or unscheduled, and whether they include mobilization or not.

In-Home Nursing Care/Mobile Nursing Services

Finding a dependable, trustworthy caregiving service while your loved one is recovering from surgery or illness can be crucial not only to their well-being, but also to your own. When you cannot hop on a plane to be there to provide comfort, support, meals, and transportation to and from doctors' appointments, you will need to hire someone who can fill your shoes.

Home health agencies offer the support needed, either 24/7 or on an hourly basis. They can even support your loved one for the long term if necessary. When you sign up for home health aide services, make sure you know exactly what services will be provided, and at what time intervals. Also find out to what extent you can count on them when facing unscheduled emergencies.

You should know that the requirements for home health aide training and certification vary by state (not that there's a lot you can do about it). Just be aware that there may be differences in credentials and then shop around to find an agency with staff that are qualified to support your elder's particular needs.

Adult Day Care/Respite Care

Adult day care centers (also called respite care centers) offer a safe environment for seniors to spend their days while providing some relief for caregivers. They incorporate a variety of age-appropriate activities that can improve health and keep your loved one moving, mentally and physically, while also curbing isolation.

These can be a great option when your elder needs more and more support with everyday life but, as a working adult, you can't be available as much as you might like. In those circumstances you might worry your parent will not be able to provide themselves with sufficient food, or that they can't structure their day independently. Respite care could offer a workable middle ground.

This kind of arrangement is ideal for a senior who needs care but still wants to live in their home environment, or one who is resistant to changing their living conditions. They can stay at the adult day care facility during the day and come back to familiar surroundings in the evening. For seniors who happen to be loners or introverts, an alternative might be an in-home aide who provides the necessary care. If money is tight, this person could be a volunteer.

Most adult day care centers are open Monday through Friday, from morning through late afternoon. They offer meals and structured activities like cognitive training, physical exercise, games, crafts, and more. You can often arrange for transportation to take your senior to and from the facility. Because respite care centers offer greater socialization than can be provided with in-home nurses or volunteers, I consider them to be a great way to battle isolation. And with the continuous care they provide, they can be the perfect solution when you want to have your cake, too.

Even though they can be the perfect link between outpatient and inpatient care, these services tend to be underutilized. For some, cost may be a limiting factor. The average out-of-pocket expense for adult day care centers is estimated at $61 per day.[3] That's a lot less than a nursing home, but it could still be prohibitive for some. Note that you and your loved one may be able to qualify for assistance through Medicaid.

Senior Living Apartment

A senior living apartment is simply an age-appropriate home that an elder occupies, either alone or together with their spouse. This type of arrangement is for the active, still-independent individual who needs a fairly low level of assistance and doesn't require nursing or medical care. Most communities offer amenities and communal services catering to an older generation, such as housekeeping, food preparation, transportation, and activities. All of these need to be arranged and paid for, of course, adding to your responsibilities and the overall costs. In other words, with a senior living apartment you might be tasked with organizing in-home care services when your elder cannot.

Note that senior living apartment should not be confused with continuing care retirement communities (CCRCs). I'll explain those later in this chapter.

If you're considering a senior living apartment setting, pay close attention to any relevant applications and terms. I came across one

---

3   "Adult Day Care," Aging in Place, modified September 2020,
    https://aginginplace.org/adult-day-care/.

that stated that spouses needed to file separate applications. Also note that most facilities will allow visits but prohibit overnight stays. That means no co-habitation with children, grandchildren, or other relatives (sorry, no couch-surfing).

In order to get into senior housing, one generally has to be at least 55 or 62 years young, depending on the development, and be willing to live around other residents who are the same age or even older. You won't find young families with small children living in these apartments. The thinking is that seniors can avoid the noise and nuisance associated with small children. That can be a valid concern, but it does give these communities a different feel. I'm not entirely convinced of the benefits.

> Dad's face would always light up when the neighbor kids rang the bell to stop by and say hello, or to play him a song as a treat. If they got too loud when they were playing in their own yard he'd chuckle and take his hearing aid out. He always said those neighbor kids made him happy because they brought fresh life to his existence. Those kids knew he had a sweet spot for them.

With that being said, senior living apartments do have some advantages. Most are designed to be wheelchair accessible and have few or no stairs. Many feature handrails, specially designed bathrooms, and other features an ordinary home might not be equipped with. In other words, they are set up to accommodate the typical needs of elderly residents.

For elderly loved ones downsizing from a large property or multi-story house, senior apartments might be a good transition. Whether your loved one wants a small studio or fancy luxury space, you can be assured their unit will be low maintenance. If you're looking for a simple way to alleviate the burden of home ownership, and if your parents don't mind being around (only) older neighbors, it might be a good option.

Personally, if my goal were to downsize and reduce home upkeep I would rather rent an apartment in a mixed-age complex for less money and use the difference to pay for whatever assistance I wanted. The extra money could be spent on home improvements, household help, takeout food, Meals on Wheels, or other forms of assistance. I happen to like kids and I'm not so sure that living exclusively among other elders is that desirable. Still, this is an option you might want to discuss with your loved one.

✳ *This option does not provide skilled nursing and medical care on-site.*

Independent Living Senior Apartment

Independent living apartments are very similar to senior living apartments. They serve a primarily elderly population and are designed for active residents desiring a maintenance-free lifestyle. The big difference is they offer a slightly greater level of care that has already been figured into the monthly rent. For example, they may provide assistance with laundry or personal transportation.

Don't assume, however, that everything your senior needs will automatically be taken care of. Before signing a lease in one of these communities, check the fine print to know what's actually included and how much of the burden will fall to the care organizer. The scheduling and coordination of activities, as well as certain aspects of assistance, might still fall in your lap. That could even result in you having to hire someone who can help out when you cannot.

✳ *This option does not provide skilled nursing and medical care on-site.*

Assisted Living Facility (ALF)

Just as the name suggests, assisted living facilities help seniors with ADLs by providing or organizing personal services. Built on a model of congregate residential living, assisted living blurs the distinction between long-term care in a senior's home and care received in an institution. For that reason you might find big variations between one place to the next when it comes to the availability of rooms versus separate apartments. Accommodations can range from single-occupancy bedrooms with private baths to ward-type rooms with communal bathroom facilities. There are also big differences in privacy, whether qualified nursing personnel are present, and (of course) cost.

It is a common misconception that assisted living facilities provide a great deal of nursing support. The reality is that most will offer residents basic hospitality, supervision, and personal services like housekeeping, meal preparation, medication reminders, and basic assistance with bathing and dressing. The vast majority partner with home health agencies to provide some level of nursing care or therapy if needed. However, round-the-clock nursing is typically not available.

If services are well managed, your involvement as a care organizer should be minimal. Just be aware that you might still need to coordinate appointments and social activities for your loved one in an assisted care facility.

Assisted living is for seniors who, in addition to wanting a low-maintenance environment, need help with basic activities. Those who require assistance bathing, walking, dressing, toileting, eating, and transferring to and from beds could be good candidates. Also, seniors living with Alzheimer's disease, or other forms of dementia, might benefit from assisted living. These facilities are not, however, for people who expect to live in them to the end regardless of changes in health or cognitive function. In most ALFs, a resident whose impairments progress and require intense nursing care for more than two weeks will be discharged from the facility.[4] It's important to read a facilities admission and retention policy carefully before signing up.

✳ *This option does not provide skilled nursing and medical care on-site.*

Naturally Occurring Retirement Community (NORC)

Naturally occurring retirement communities are like assisted living in a village with other seniors. They have popped up in places where younger people have moved away, leaving self-sustained neighbor-

---

4   Catherine Hawes, Ph.D., Miriam Rose, M.Ed., and Charles D. Phillips, Ph.D., M.P.H., "A National Study of Assisted Living for the Frail Elderly: Results of a National Survey of Facilities," December 14, 1999, https://aspe.hhs.gov/basic-report/national-study-assisted-living-frail-elderly-results-national-survey-facilities.

hoods with residents who were mainly age 60 and over. These areas feature almost endless amenities and social activities, assuming residents can finance and manage them. From transportation services to grocery stores, household chore assistance, home health care, and more, everything is available on an as-needed basis.

NORCs are usually financed by some mix of public and private funding. They may receive government support or draw on charitable contributions, and function from corporate or nonprofit partnerships. One of the things that makes this kind of arrangement unique is the wide variety of services available (to the community or the individual) based on need, budget, and preference.

It's worth noting that some "naturally occurring" retirement communities are actually privately financed and operated. Whether a community you are considering is the result of generational change or business planning, you should always do your homework before making lifestyle decisions with your loved one.

Buying into a Continuing Care Retirement Community (CCRC)

Buying into a continuing care retirement community (or CCRC) is hands down the ideal arrangement for a senior who wants to age in place. Here is how it works: your senior purchases a new home within a network of different types of housing and service options. The property types might range from condominiums to single-family homes, and care services go from zero care (i.e., independent living) all the way to advanced or hospice choices.

If you have the financial means to pursue this option, you have lots of choices. In fact, this market is expanding so quickly, and the options are so dependent on personal preferences and budgets, that I won't even go into details. What matters is that the level of care can always be adjusted. For example, if your loved one requires a higher level of attention, they can transition from a home or apartment to a nursing facility and still be close to a spouse or family. Friends from the same community can easily come visit, even as these transitions take place. The social aspect of these communities is almost priceless.

Ideally, your loved one could begin the transition to a CCRC while they are relatively fit and independent. Before they buy in, though, it's important to read documentation carefully and realize that if the on-site facility is full the elder may have to go elsewhere to an open bed and wait for open space to return. Be sure to ask how often this happens and be prepared to receive a vague answer.

Board and Care Homes

For an elderly family member who needs special care due to physical issues, cognitive impairment, or even more serious dementia or Alzheimer's, group homes staffed with trained personnel can be a safe choice.

Board and care homes are different from other assisted living options in that daily schedules tend to be less structured, giving residents more independence. Most will have 24-hour staffing by professional care providers, as well as personal services on premises. The best ones feel more like homes and less like institutions, which can be important for seniors to be comfortable in their surroundings.

One other advantage of board and care homes is that they can be less expensive than larger senior communities. With costs in the $3,000–$5,000-per-month range, they aren't cheap but still offer some savings against other choices.

✱ Most group homes do not provide round-the-clock skilled nursing and medical care on-site, but some do. Look into the details before making any decisions.

Nursing Care Homes

A nursing care facility (also called a skilled nursing facility, convalescent home, or "old folks home") is an institution providing care and medical assistance 24 hours a day, seven days a week. Nursing care may be provided in the short term, for example for rehabilitation from surgery, or long term, such as when permanent custodial assistance and ongoing medical care are required. Some facilities have a doctor on staff, or will be connected to a network of physicians who take house calls. Facilities are legally required to have at least one registered nurse

(RN) on staff, but many nursing care homes will employ several who can not only assist with everyday tasks but also dispense medications to patients (as per doctor's orders).

One of the crucial ingredients of happiness for an elderly person is finding a living situation that facilitates social engagement and gives a sense of purpose and belonging. A major (and often-ignored) drawback of having your loved one remain in their own home is the lack of contact with others, which can lead to isolation and depression. This is important to remember because nursing home facilities have a reputation for maintaining an atmosphere that can almost be described as hospital-like. They certainly can feel that way, but they also give seniors plenty of chances to make friends and be involved.

In a typical nursing care home, patients will reside in a single room with a private bath. In some cases, though, they may share a room and bathroom. Each room is typically equipped with a hospital bed, nightstand, closet, chair, and a table. Some nursing homes will allow you to bring your own furniture and decorations. If you choose one that does, take advantage of it and make a cozy nest for your loved one. Just don't fill it too much – you'll want cleaning staff and medical personnel to be able to get around without any problems.

Nursing home residents take their meals together in a dining room, except in cases where health conditions prevent them from doing so. The home will offer scheduled activities like cognitive and physical training, singing, crafts, and group outings. This can be valuable for you as the care organizer, since it takes the burden of planning from you and lets you finally relax.

If time allows, look at as many nursing homes as you can. Get used to the atmosphere of each one and pick up on the nuances. And remember, when your loved one has become disabled, or needs constant medical care and cannot safely live at home, the move into a nursing home is warranted.

✳ *Nursing homes provide round-the-clock skilled nursing and medical care on-site.*

Memory Care Facility

A memory care facility is a special type of skilled nursing home, assisted living facility, or residential care home. In these places, specific types of assistance and daily care planning for memory-challenged patients are offered. Because services vary, you will need to check with the facility you are evaluating to see if they have specialized caregivers on staff.

For example, some facilities offer a closed memory care unit for patients who exhibit tendencies of wandering – a typical behavior in advanced cases of dementia or Alzheimer's. Some other so-called open homes will take patients with mild forms of dementia but have strict policies like "three strikes and you're out" when it comes to walking off the premises unattended. Harsh as it might seem, those kinds of rules are there for the safety of patients. If your loved one has a tendency to wander away, you should look into a closed memory care home from the start so you won't have to go through the trouble of moving them more than once.

Your choice of memory care facility will alternately depend on the progression of your loved one's disease, your preferences, and your available budget.

❋ *These facilities provide round-the-clock skilled nursing and medical care on-site.*

Palliative or Hospice Care

It's important for you, as the care organizer, to know what your loved one's wishes are for end-of-life care. If they are facing a terminal illness, do they want to receive life-preserving treatments for as long as possible in the hope for a cure, or to stop treatment and receive end-of-life care for pain management so they can live out their last days at home?

Depending on the circumstances, and their wishes, palliative care or hospice care can improve the quality of life for elders and their family members. The main difference between the two is that in palliative care the patient continues his or her treatment, while in hospice care only pain and symptoms are addressed.

Palliative care can be given to anyone battling a serious illness or dealing with complications from an accident. A multidisciplinary team will help the senior and their family to understand the choices. However, if the patient understands their illness is no longer responding to medical treatment, or they are facing a disease and progress cannot be slowed, they might wish to receive hospice care instead.

In hospice, patients and families get the emotional and spiritual support they need when facing certain death. This is no small thing; terminally ill patients and their family members need all the help they can get. The goal of hospice is to minimize the patient's pain and suffering while maintaining their dignity and self-determination, thus providing a loving and caring environment during the end-of-life stage.

✳ *Both palliative care and hospice care can be provided in hospitals, nursing homes, specialized clinics, or at home.*

Making the Right Call

There is no one-size-fits-all solution when it comes to senior care options, if only for the simple reason that we all have different needs and preferences. Figuring out what's right for your loved one depends on many factors, some of which may change over time.

Perhaps your senior isn't quite ready to move into a skilled nursing home. For someone who has always lived a physically or mentally active life, keeping that up for as long as possible (or replacing activities and interests with new ones) will be very important. Going to adult day care could be a great way to keep those parts of their lives intact while also giving you the peace of mind that comes with knowing your loved one is supervised and not alone. So long as they aren't struggling with an array of health issues, keeping your senior in their home, organizing a home health aide, and utilizing daytime assistance could be a great choice.

Are you intrigued by the facility with great amenities, fun activities, and even daily bed-making? That kind of arrangement might seem like a "hands-off" solution for you, but check the fine print. There might be a lot for you to do even after your loved one has moved in. Ask yourself: "If my parent moved into this community or facility, in what sense would it be different? Is that a major improvement from the current situation?" No matter what the answer is, it's important to know what you are signing up for *before* you commit.

Finances can be another major consideration. It's important to take the time to understand in detail what services are included in the base price you're quoted for any facility or care level, as well as which extras and amenities are not. Then, you can see for yourself what will realistically be left for you to pay out of pocket.

> Prepare early to secure a spot because the good places fill up quickly.

Be aware that most senior care providers and facilities have a rather long wait list. The sooner you can begin to narrow down your choices, the better. Your aim should be to get your name on the waiting list of as many potential destinations as possible, even if the move isn't imminent. You never know when you will need a spot for your loved one and you don't want to rush the decision when the time comes.

And finally, remember that your ultimate goal is a better situation for your loved one and yourself. Keep that in front of your mind when contemplating new living quarters for the senior in your life. But also remember that what might look good in your own vision of the future might not sound as appealing to them.

Personally, I hope to see more communities naturally create the kind of support systems needed to help an aging population. I can imagine myself living in a real NORC someday – a neighborhood where I'm surrounded by my friends, and where we can pool our resources to set up a self-governing structure to help each other out as we get older. I am hopeful the growing number of Baby Boomers will shape this sector for the better in the coming years. In fact, I'd be willing to bet almost anything that we will see new, exciting, and innovative approaches in senior care and housing as time rolls on.

Whether your elder is staying at home and hiring a caregiver or residing in a nursing home community, you will have monthly expenses you did not have before.

Can We Afford It?

The Many Ways to Pay for Senior Housing and Care

For most, financial considerations will BE the biggest factor when deciding on housing and care solutions. With that in mind, it pays to know your budget and to plan ahead by learning about (and accounting for) any hidden costs *before* you move your senior to a new home.

As an example, residents of skilled nursing facilities often pay extra for services like medication administration, transportation, and assistance with daily activities or nursing care that goes above and beyond the minimum covered by the basic rate of the home. You could argue that this isn't necessarily a bad thing; why would you want to pay for services your loved one might never use? That's a valid argument, but most of us hate surprise expenses. It's much better to understand the fine print on any contract you sign before the bills start showing up.

You'll want to know exactly how often, and by how much, management can raise the rent, as well as which costs are covered in monthly payments. Prices tend to rise over time, and you need to know whether these fun bus tours your loved one wants to partake in are included – not just now but also down the road. To complete your financial plan you must also figure in your budget the cost for supplemental insurance, out-of-pocket spending on health care medications, and basic needs like personal items or clothing so you don't fall short.

Where You Live Matters

From small to large, modest to plush, the choices in senior housing are plenty, both here in the US and abroad. You can rent or buy, and prices will vary greatly from one state to another. They may even be much different within different areas of the same communities.

While I can't give you concrete figures on costs, I can tell you that money is a constant fact of life at any stage. Just as a younger person must decide where to live based on income and financial resources, so will a senior. This may mean your loved one has to broaden their horizons and consider a change of scenery away from familiar surroundings. These changes can be difficult for an older person to accept, but their cost of living can change dramatically from one state or region to the next.

The first thing you need to consider with your elderly loved one is what type of home or apartment will be best suited for their budget, lifestyle, health care needs, and expectations. If you are looking for lower costs and low maintenance, an apartment in a lower-cost neighborhood (or even a different state) might be a good choice. If you have a bigger budget with bigger tastes to match, then you might consider something larger.

As with anything else in life, your choices will be largely guided by your financial resources. Let's look at some of the options and resources you might consider:

Low-Income Rentals

If you meet certain income criteria determined by state and federal agencies, you might be able to rent an affordable senior living apartment at below-market rates. These units are subsidized by public funds, meaning they generally cost less than other properties in the area but require applicants to show they have a financial need.

Have you checked to see whether your relative qualifies for HUD-sponsored senior housing? Visit the department of Housing and Urban Development Website at **HUD.gov** for eligibility requirements. Shared housing with another senior can be another economical alternative. To find opportunities, visit **nationalsharedhousing.org.**

Below-Market-Rate Rentals

Conventional rental rates are usually set as high as the market will bear. However, rents for income-based housing can be well below local rates (sometimes as much as 15% lower). To find these opportunities, check within your local community and visit the websites for municipal resource centers. There you can find information on these kinds of housing arrangements, as well as what criteria you and your senior might have to meet to qualify.

Keep in mind that some income-based housing for seniors includes additional services like community dining, as well as assistance with housekeeping and transportation.

Luxury Rentals

Does size matter to you? If money is no issue and you want your loved one to spend the rest of their life in style, the luxury senior housing market has lots to offer. From 2,000-plus-square-foot homes or apartments to upscale amenities and fancy events, the world can be your oyster – if you are prepared to pay.

Paying for Care

The leading companies in the senior housing and care industry all have a few things in common: they have invested heavily in the structure of their communities, marketed their home health services to millions, and have become increasingly popular. One might conclude that given the highly competitive nature of this market prices would be leveling off. Ironically, though, they continue to be on the rise.

According to Genworth's Cost of Care Survey (2019)[5], the average costs for care are steep:

- A private room in a nursing home in the United States runs a staggering $8,517 per month. That comes out to $279 each and every day.

- The average cost of assisted living comes in at $4,051 per month, or $133 per day.

- The cost of a home health aide averages out at $4,385 per month, or $144 per day.

These numbers don't get any smaller when you add them up over time. The average annual cost of that private room in a nursing home? It was $102,200 in 2019, and is projected to skyrocket to $137,348 by 2029.

These rates are largely out of reach for most older persons unless they happen to be independently wealthy and can tap into their assets by liquidating them. That leads us to the million-dollar question…

So How Are We Going to Pay for This? This is by far the hardest nut to crack. Now that you know long-term care costs are high to begin with, and can easily take a bigger chunk out of an elder's pocket than originally estimated, it's time to get into the details. That means talking money, and possibly even relocation options, with your loved one and ensuring funding is in place for housing and care.

Don't get discouraged. I've given you some big numbers, but you might not have to foot the entire bill. Let's look at some potential sources of funding.

5   "Cost of Care Survey," Genworth, last modified March 3, 2020,
    https://www.genworth.com/aging-and-you/finances/cost-of-care.html.

Housing Subsidies

Seniors who qualify for HUD subsidies can receive Section 8 Housing Choice Vouchers and use them to pay all or part of their rent in privately owned apartments or public housing communities. Guidelines vary from state to state, and even within districts, so check within your community to see whether you qualify to receive one of these vouchers to pay for rent and utilities.

Given that this program often has a long waiting list, it's a good idea to prepare all paperwork quickly and carefully to speed up the application process. Note that special provisions are in place for expedited approval in cases where a senior is homeless or living in an unsafe environment.

If you have questions about your senior's situation or eligibility, you can talk to a HUD-approved housing counselor. You can also visit the HUD website for information on housing for elderly residents in your state, or contact a local elder care case management organization. These nonprofits can often assist families in navigating the application process.

Keep in mind that if your senior has assets in their name that could be considered as (or converted to) income they may not qualify for HUD housing. As tempting as it might be to transfer these assets into the name of a family member to squeeze below the threshold for subsidies, I would strongly advise you to consult with an elder care case manager or attorney first. They can help you come up with a solid financial strategy and keep you from making costly mistakes.

The AHEPA National Housing Corporation

AHEPA is a nonprofit organization based in Fishers, Indiana, and devoted to helping senior citizens find housing that offers regular on-site medical services and nutritional programs. Their services are free, but eligibility for their programs is based on income or disability.

AHEPA currently manages 94 properties in 21 states. Search their website **ahepahousing.org** for details or to submit an application for your senior.

Medicare

Medicare may help with housing and treatment costs, but is generally only available for a limited time and may not apply to many circumstances. For instance, Medicare Part A only pays for rehab and skilled long-term care services in a Medicare-certified nursing home, and only for a maximum of 100 days. Even then, it's only applicable if your senior was admitted within 30 days of treatment at the hospital. Any costs associated with longer stays need to be paid for out of pocket.

Medicare may conditionally pay for a limited amount of at-home care, but will not cover activities of daily living services. For more information on Medicare coverage, visit **https://www.medicare.gov/coverage/skilled-nursing-facility-snf-care**. There are also excellent planning resources at **LongTermCare.gov** and **https://www.genworth.com/aging-and-you/finances/cost-of-care.html**. Just be aware that specific links may change over time.

Medicaid

In contrast to Medicare, Medicaid pays for the majority of long-term care services for seniors with limited financial resources. Eligibility is based on modified adjusted gross income (MAGI) and is tied to the federal poverty level. Benefits vary from state to state, and enrollment and renewal processes change periodically. Check **Medicaid.gov** for up-to-date information.

VA Benefits

Veterans may be eligible for assistance through the Department of Veterans Affairs (VA) benefit program, which covers costs for in-home care or boarding at care homes. Visit **va.gov/health** for more information, or to download the latest federal benefits guide.

Private Long-Term Care Insurance

These policies can often be used to cover care and some services. Discuss this form of supplemental health insurance with your financial advisor to examine costs and maximize future benefits.

Private Funding

If your elder doesn't meet low-income requirements it might be necessary to get creative and start looking at private funding approaches. Supplemental funds to help cover long-term care costs could come from the sale of an existing home, interest and dividends from investments, or income from rental properties.

Many seniors do not want to deplete their life savings, and may wish to leave some assets to surviving family members after their passing. Here are some options you and your loved one might want to discuss with a financial advisor or elder care lawyer in order to find the most sensible solution:

- Private or family pay
- Estate replacement plans
- Long-term care insurance
- Reverse mortgages
- Life insurance options
- Annuities
- Advanced inheritance plans
- Shared inheritance plans
- Family contracts
- Lifetime estates
- Charitable remainder trusts
- Lifetime property interests
- Supplemental needs trusts

> "Don't design this plan alone. Work with someone who has received specific and extensive training in this area.

Financial Assistance: It Never Hurts to Ask

In the unfortunate event you discover your loved one's funds are tight – or simply nonexistent – you may find yourself looking at financing options or various forms of financial aid. The earlier you start exploring them, the better. There may still be time to get the money side of things in order before the need for care arises.

Take full advantage of public and private benefits programs. Federal, state, and local government initiatives all exist to help older individuals pay for expenses such as doctors' visits, transportation, food, energy bills, and property taxes. There are more than 2,500 of these programs available nationwide. Visit your local county office to learn about available programs and understand all the details before you commit to any housing decision.

Finding Current Information on Programs for Seniors

It is above and beyond the scope of this book to attempt to cover the details of these many programs. Rather than give incomplete information, I will refer you to the website of the National Council on Aging at **benefitscheckup.org**. Once you're there, you can enter your ZIP Code to quickly get results on senior benefit packages that may interest you and your loved one. The service is free, and you may be pleasantly surprised at what is available.

The one option I have found particularly useful, and that might be especially helpful to you as a care organizer, is the Respite Program. Earlier, I introduced you to adult day care services, which are a good example of this type of service. They are designed to give caregivers much-needed relief. Even if you are only organizing care for your elder, you still might be able to make use of respite care, particularly when you find yourself burnt out or in a pickle.

Another especially helpful online resource is **payingforseniorcare. com**. The goal of this website is to find the means to pay for senior care by providing objective information and interactive tools on a platform that is easy to use and advertisement-free. Here you will find insights about the types of senior care, costs and how to pay for them, a resource locator tool, another tool that compares benefits and care, and much more. There are sections about planning for care, advice on how to find affordable senior services, tips on lowering costs, cost-saving technologies, and even FAQs. You'll also find links to helpful guides and paid caregiver programs.

You might also check out **totalseniorsavings.com**. Its information program is designed to help low-income, uninsured, and underserved patients who need help paying for all or part of their medical care. It turns out most insurance companies offer medical financial assistance programs for qualifying patients who need help with emergency or medically necessary care. Who would have thought? See if your elder meets the eligibility requirements to enroll.

You can find more information on senior living prices at **seniorly. com** and **senioradvisor.com**. Both have great information and easy search functions.

And finally, no description of resources would be complete without mentioning the American Association of Retired Persons. Everyone has heard of AARP, and I can almost guarantee you got an invitation to join once you turned 50.

Check out their membership program at **aarp.org** to learn more about their programs and benefits, including the **AARP Foundation**. Its mission is security, protection, and empowerment for older persons in need. They also have links to informative articles and all kinds of discounts for members.

Once you start to get a sense of what's out there, and how your senior could benefit, there are a few more resources you might want to check out:

- The Administration on Aging
- The National Institute on Aging
- The Alzheimer's Association
- The American Association of Homes and Services for the Aging
- The Assisted Living Federation of America
- The American Seniors Housing Association
- The American Health Care Association
- National Center for Assisted Living

Remember: everyone's situation is different and circumstances can change in a heartbeat. The sooner you begin your search, the better you will fare. Don't wait until it's too late.

Only your loved one knows what the most important factors are for their happiness and well-being. Listen carefully to them so you can find out what really matters in their life and respect their wishes for as long as possible.

What's Your Pick?

Making the Choice on Where Your Senior Should Live

I hope that by this point in the process you have already had "the talk" with your loved one and feel they are ready to listen to your suggestions. Together you will have to make a decision on how and where they want to spend the rest of their lives. Assuming you have carefully assessed the situation, read and acted on the previous chapters, and presented the findings to your senior, you should be ready to narrow down the choices.

The key is to initiate a conversation that will define their new way of living, but doing so without any pressure. With the caveat that you should always prioritize safety before comfort, let your elderly loved one decide how they want to live. Really *listen carefully* to what matters most to them.

If your mom or dad's biggest pleasure is relaxing in a cozy chair in total privacy, for example, you might prioritize a senior living facility with a home health aide service that can give them the space and solitude they crave. Placing them in an institutionalized setting with communal dining, and maybe even shared bathrooms, would be quite upsetting.

What makes sense on paper doesn't always fit as nicely with someone else's idea of comfort. So long as it's possible and reasonable you should accommodate their wishes.

> **So which one is it: home, sweet home, or a new living arrangement?**

It took me quite some time to research and develop a carefully thought-out strategy. I was both eager and anxious to present it to my parents.

My father listened reluctantly, but did allow me to show him the information I had gathered. Knowing he wanted to die in the house he built, and that he was too vain to even be seen using a walker, it was obvious to me which direction I had to go. My plan was to send Dad to adult day care so Mom would get a break from caregiving, and to arrange a home health aide to assist with things like injections and personal hygiene.

When I broke the news to Dad that a nurse would be coming to bathe him, he chuckled and asked: "Is that right? A cute 20-year-old is going to see me naked?" I was relieved – at least he found some humor in what was going to be a major intrusion on his privacy.

The one time you can ignore your loved one's wishes is when their own safety (or another person's safety) is in jeopardy. When that happens, the consequence may be that they have to move out of a comfortable home into unfamiliar surroundings. However, that does *not* necessarily mean your elder can't ever be comfortable again. Make sure to get that point across when talking about these issues. Even though I wanted my father to be happy, I would not have given into his demands if I had any worry about whether he and my mother were at serious risk for an accident or injury.

If there's no urgency to find a new living solution right away, you can simply write down some notes from your conversation and set the topic aside for a future date. On the other hand, if you both conclude that something needs to change soon, you might need to get moving quickly. Either way, you may wish to be proactive and begin with a few adjustments to your loved one's existing living quarters or start searching for a new home if it's going to save you time and stress later.

As you'll discover, most seniors prefer to age in place in a home where they already settled and comfortable. We will look at how you can help them to stay put safely in the next chapter.

So your loved one has decided to age in place. That means you'll need to take a closer look at the current living space and make sure their sweet abode can serve their growing needs for years to come.

Home, Sweet Home

Setting the Stage for Aging in Place

M ost older adults are understandably afraid of losing control over their lives. They absolutely dread the thought of living a lonely, disconnected, and isolated existence in an unfamiliar place. Adding to that misery is the fear of going broke. Does $8,500+ a month sound like something you can easily afford?

It's no wonder more and more folks want to remain in their homes long into their golden years. As long as the environment is safe, and the home is comfortable and easy to take care of with an age-appropriate layout, having a fairly independent adult age in place isn't a bad choice.

Some people manage quite well on their own as they get older without ever needing to hire nursing staff. There is a lot to be said for being able to perform daily tasks for as long as possible. It keeps the body, mind, and spirit alive. How feasible that is depends a great deal on three things: how used to living independently an elder is, the personal connections they have with others (like friendly neighbors), and the setup within the home. You probably can't control those first two variables, but you can take charge of the last one.

Agreeing to an in-home care arrangement for your loved one in a house that is not senior proof isn't a good idea. In fact, it's a disaster waiting to happen.

A Checklist to Help Determine a Home's Suitability for Aging in Place:

- Is the home safe and is the layout age-appropriate (free of narrow staircases, etc.)?

- Is the home easy to take care of and maintain?

- Is there a full bathroom, bedroom, and kitchen all on one floor level?

- Is the shower/tub/toilet easily accessible and slip proof?

- Does the bathroom meet the needs of the senior?

- Are there grab bars in the bathroom, or can you add them?

- Does the home have stairs or an elevator? Can you add a lift?

- Could you make the home handicap accessible?

- How close is the home to shopping and activities? Within walking distance or further?

- Are there walking trails or sidewalks nearby?

- Is the neighborhood safe?

- Is parking safe and convenient? Is it close by and well lit at night?

- Are there safety features like a 24-hour alert system, smoke detectors, or sprinkler system?

- Is storage space easily accessible?

- Are the counters and cupboards convenient for your senior?

- Could you hire housekeeping and other help?

- Is it easy to prepare or get food?

Your senior's home didn't quite make the cut? Let's see what you can do about it. Skip to **Home Smarts,** later in this chapter, where I will show you which modifications you can make for senior living setup. When the home is safe and your loved one is physically and mentally able to remain there alone, you might not have to look very far to seal the deal on continuing care. Who knows? You may have everything you need except a pet!

Once the aging process has made it too difficult to perform routine household chores, hiring someone to clean and do laundry will make daily living much easier for your loved one. The same holds true for ordering takeout or signing up for service like Meals on Wheels. Senior citizens often rebuff these ideas out of pride, financial concerns, or both. What they may not realize is the money spent on those small luxuries isn't much when compared to the cost of a nursing home. Every year they stay in their own property, they are saving more money than they might realize.

In-home care, also called mobile nursing services, can provide seniors with home health assistance, non-medical care, and even personal enrichment programs tailored to your loved one's personal interests. Care can be as minimal as one hour a day or a few hours a week. Or, it can be more comprehensive. There are even some full-time services.

> I successfully used this argument with my mom. She is all about saving money.

With these arrangements in place, the provider comes to the home to help with things like dressing, bathing, and preparing meals. They may also monitor heart rate and blood pressure, administer insulin injections, and do even more depending on what is needed. Services vary greatly from one provider to the next, and may or may not include visits from a physician, physician's assistant, or nurse practitioner. Some incorporate physical therapists, occupational therapists, or home health nurses.

A mobile caregiver is usually *not* someone who lives with the patient unless the patient requires full-time assistance due to Alzheimer's or severe physical disability.

It pays to compare service providers and ask for referrals within your personal social circles, as well as the larger community. I found that hiring non-medical care services (like household help) through nursing care providers meant paying a premium. Unless you are looking for a one-stop shop when it comes to adult care, you might be better off organizing medical and non-medical services separately.

Where to Find Care Providers (and What to Watch Out For)

The mobile nursing service is a booming industry, and in most areas you can find multiple in-home care services for hire. A quick search within your community will yield a list of providers, and possibly even some interesting nonprofit-guided volunteer programs offering assistance to seniors. These can be a wonderful resource when funds are tight and you need basic care.

While it's safer to contract with a fully insured and bonded agency, you could check out online portals to find a helping hand for temporary or fill-in needs. I lucked out and found household help for my mom in Germany by using the internet. I found a gardener the same way. I would caution you to pay the extra expense for a background check, though, so you don't end up with a psycho or crook in your parents' home. Trust your instincts and pay attention if anything seems suspicious. And when in doubt, stick to a reputable home health care agency that belongs to the National Association of Home Care and Hospice (**nahc.org**).

Hiring help means you now have another person to manage, in addition to yourself and your parent. You are in a sense becoming an employer and personnel manager all at once. That can be a challenge.

I had to nail down the details of in-home care. I wanted to find a service with compassionate, reliable staff members – someone my parents would be happy and comfortable with. After all, these strangers would be entering our family home freely, at any given time, and performing very intimate tasks.

When trying to figure out what my parents really needed, I constantly asked myself: "Is this actually helping them, or is the intrusion into their privacy not worth it? What should I watch out for? What am I forgetting?"

Insist on meeting some of the caregiving staff before you sign a contract with any service provider. The people managing the business rarely get involved in the day-to-day duties. It's important, for your own peace of mind, to know that the caregiving staff will be 100% trustworthy, loving, and respectful of the patients they look after. The person looking after your loved one should encourage social interactions while helping the senior to remain calm in anxious situations. They should build rapport with your loved one over time and be observant of changes in their mental or physical health.

Communication is an important aspect of the caregiver's role that is easy to overlook. The person who is interacting with your loved one on a day-to-day basis should communicate clearly with them. They should also report back to you regularly. If they don't do that automatically (as my mother's caregivers do) then it's on you to check in with them, as well as your elderly parent, at regular intervals.

All it takes is one bad apple to ruin an elder's day. If that happens you're bound to hear about it for weeks and months to come. Think about the difference it makes for your loved one to have a regular visit they look forward to with someone who will be there to hold their hand and care about them. And then think about what would be missing from their life without those interactions.

While we are on the subject of social interactions, let me point out that an in-home care or mobile care service provider will send someone who comes to your senior's home and leaves once their tasks have been completed. So, depending on the level of assistance required, these visits may be short in nature. If your loved one feels lonely, hiring a caregiver is not going to be the answer to that problem; you will need to look for additional opportunities for social connection. In those instances you might schedule and manage social activities for your parent, find a volunteer companion who can spend some time with them, or enroll them at an adult day care center.

Your loved one's circumstances will dictate what kind of help is required, and it's likely their requirements will change over time. Make sure you find the appropriate help for the situation your elder is facing. Let's say, for example, that your senior's home is a nightmare to maintain, and that even with modifications it won't be safe. Under those circumstances getting in-home nursing care just won't be enough. Know what can and can't work so you can change course as needed.

When my mother's eyesight deteriorated I thought for sure she would need to move out of her house. But when I consulted her ophthalmologist, he advised her to stay in her familiar environment for as long as possible, even though the house was less than ideal. His reasoning was that because Mom had lived most of her life in that home, she knew every single step. She was familiar with every nook and cranny, which was a huge advantage when compared to a potentially new environment where she would have to find her way around without knowing the lay of the land. His reassurance made me put aside my doubts.

Some inexpensive modifications to the home made it possible for her to stay there for a few more years. We made sure there were no places where she could get caught, or slip and fall, by getting rid of the many layers of rugs and checking the threshold in each doorway. We changed the lighting throughout the house and added LED strips under and inside cabinets or drawers. We also placed small rubberized tabs on the stove, refrigerator door, microwave, freezer, washer/dryer, and other appliances so she could "feel" the settings instead of seeing them. I bought her a speaking alarm clock, touchable nightlight, a telephone with huge buttons, and a digital reading device from Optelec. The total cost of these modifications was no more than $200, not including the reading device. That thing sure was pricey, but when she no longer needed it I was able to recoup some of the investment by selling it.

For the bathtub she had a lift – a nifty invention that could safely lower her inside for bathing. Showering would have been possible, but not advisable, due to the risk of dizzy spells. Handlebars were already installed in all the right places in the bathroom, so we only needed to make a toilet seat height adjustment.

To ensure Mom could get help in an emergency we had a 24/7 emergency call system installed. They gave her a slick-looking panic button that she wore day and night on her wrist. Those devices were fully waterproof and could be worn even when bathing. As it turned out, those were the times when seniors were most likely to activate them. We made sure Mom knew that and didn't take it off before her bath.

After these adjustments were made, we hired help for cleaning, garden, and house maintenance. We organized a nurse to stop by and administer medication. Her primary care physician started stopping by the house from time to time. Most importantly, we found her a companion to visit every week.

All in all, Mom was set. The last item on the agenda was to figure out how to curb her loneliness. She felt terribly isolated after her husband of 66 years had passed. Adult day care to the rescue!

Adult Day Care/Respite Care

What happens after a home health aide has left your senior's home? In my opinion this is a critical time, and one that's easy to ignore or overlook.

Once you have completed your research on home improvements or care services, I would encourage you to take the next step and look at programs geared toward socialization for elders. You want to make sure your loved one does not feel isolated, and that any long gaps between visits are filled.

For example, imagine a situation where a nurse comes to your parent's home in the mornings and evenings to help with bathing, dressing, and medication. How will your parent spend the time between those visits? Will they be alone? In most situations that's *exactly* what happens. The elder finds their day is filled with waiting for the nurse to show up again. There might be a couple of phone calls here and there, or a little bit of TV and reading. If that's the sum of their life, going day in and day out with no personal interactions, it's going to be depressing. It's certainly not how I would envision spending my golden years! I bet you feel the same way.

Adult day care is a wonderful solution in my opinion. By attending a senior-focused facility, elders who are no longer capable of remaining home alone on a full-time basis can spend the day away in a safe and caring environment.

Most adult day care centers have programs that are designed to nurture and challenge members, and to get them involved in stimulating activities throughout the day. That daily structure, along with the mental and physical stimulation provided, can increase the quality of life for your loved one and allow them to live at home longer.

Adult day care centers are not only safe places for seniors to spend the day and socialize with others, but they also provide a respite – a rare slice of peace of mind – for any caregiver or care organizer. And best of all, they won't break the bank.

My dad went to adult day care and gave my mom a break from caregiving. After he passed away and Mom got too lonely, it felt very natural for her to go to the same place as well. She already knew the staff members in the facility, and because everyone already knew Dad they were very welcoming to her.

For me it was a great relief knowing that my mother was under supervision for most of the day. Whenever I called, she would tell me a story about things that happened at the center. Some were good and some were bad. It turned out that even with her eyesight issues she was the fittest of the group, both mentally and physically. At times she wished for more challenging activities.

One of her favorite complaints was the singing hour. "How many times do I have to sing the stupid song 'Hoch auf dem gelben Wagen'?" Apparently she had gotten tired of the old German childhood tunes. I wholeheartedly agreed, so I brought it up with management and a couple of weeks later the repertoire had been replaced with music from the '70s. It even got some of the folks dancing... my mom included!

Clearing the Clutter

It's not uncommon to find that the only thing making a home unsafe for an older person is clutter. Holding on to too many things, and not storing them properly, can cause falls that could otherwise easily be avoided. So, before you can even begin making modifications to your senior's home, know that you might have to roll up your sleeves and get rid of a bunch of stuff.

My father was a borderline hoarder. No one was allowed to touch any of his stuff. Most of it lived in the basement.

According to Dad, there was a system to his madness. And, to give him credit, whenever he needed some obscure item it would usually take him less than a few minutes to produce it. Before he would hand it over to you he would dangle it in front of your face with this big grin and say, "MY organization... see?"

After Dad's funeral my mom declared she wanted everything gone, except for a few precious items that reminded her of her husband. I started with his closet. Dad's clothes were donated or given away. All in all, it didn't take long to clean it out. He was a modest man and didn't indulge. It's hard to describe, but it was a strange sensation to touch and handle the clothes he wore. But I knew it was important for my mother to get closure. She – not me – still had to live in the house without him. We even found a drop box for his eyeglasses at the optometrist. I was told they could repurpose prescription lenses, which I thought was very cool.

Finally, we got to the basement. It was unbelievable what he had stashed in there. There was a little bit of everything, from plumbing supplies to his favorite magazines. How could I forget to mention brand-new shoes he had once bought on sale (at least 10 pairs), or the swimming pool ladder that went to a pool we had never owned? There was even one(!) very long ski pole that would fit a person well over six feet tall. It looked to be some sort of wooden antique. Dad was five foot four and didn't ski. To this day I wonder how he got a hold of it and why he kept it.

Clearing out that basement took more than a month. First, I had to somehow wrap my head around Dad's organization system and then create my own. Luckily, he had a habit of storing things in boxes, and there were tons of empty ones lying around that I was able to use. I gathered a bunch of sticky notes and markers and got to work. One box for hardware, another for paints and brushes, a third for old birthday cards... you get the idea.

The challenge was dealing with the space, or maybe I should say the lack thereof, while trying to figure out what was useful and what was not. I didn't want to just throw everything in the dump. I asked myself: what if there were something valuable or necessary in the pile? Then, a second (or possibly worse) thought came to me: was I starting to think just like him?

Luckily, Mom always seemed to sense just when I needed a break. She would call for me and present me with a cup of hot coffee and a little cake for kaffeeklatsch. I still remember marching upstairs and showing her the solitary ski pole. We both laughed hysterically, a priceless moment we both needed so much.

Home Smarts

Let's hope you don't have to get rid of extensive clutter like I did. Either way, once it's gone you can dive right in and address the most important area in the home...

Floors

To make a home safe for a senior, all area rugs and loose flooring need to be removed or tacked down. Why? These are the *number one* hazard that cause older people to trip and fall. Floors should be either wall-to-wall carpeted, hardwood, laminate, or vinyl without anything placed on top. You might want to pay attention to the type of shoes your elder wears inside the house, as well. Some shoes with stickier soles can actually be worse for so-called "shufflers." Make sure the ones your senior wears are just sticky enough to prevent them from slipping, but not so much that they'll get caught and cause a trip.

It was hard to convince my mother we had to rip out all the old worn carpet and layers of area rugs she had piled on top of it. She didn't think the home would be cozy enough, and worried she might miss her comfort. But after I installed nice grippy vinyl flooring in a warm color and bought her some house slippers that were comfortable, low heeled, and properly fitting, she adapted quickly.

Along with slippery bathroom tiles, seniors are often injured by loose cables or extension cords. The cord that connects that beloved La-Z-Boy to the wall needs to be securely fastened so no one can trip over it. Also inspect door thresholds closely and be sure there are no corners or edges sticking up (something that is more likely to happen in an older home). You should also repair any transition changes on floors.

For the purposes of safety, anything you put on top of the floor might as well be the floor itself. For example, that comfy bathmat might feel nice on your feet as you get in the shower, but if it doesn't have a non-slip bottom it can become a flying carpet in a hurry. A better solution for a bathroom floor – not to mention a tub or shower – is a set of anti-slip stickers. I bought mine in the children's section from IKEA. They look a bit... *cute,* but they work perfectly because they come in contrasting colors so they are easy for my mother to see. Also make sure to keep a mop, and paper towels, next to any water sources to wipe away spills from the floor promptly.

If the home where your senior will be living has two or more stories, you also need to ensure the staircase has a non-slip surface and that, just like any other floor in the house, any carpet is securely attacked with loose edges fastened.

Let There Be Light!

Having enough light in the right places, without glare, makes a home safer for an elderly person. It can also make it easier for them to find things that seem hidden in drawers or closets. Make Thomas Edison proud and don't skip on the wattage.

To check the lighting in your senior's home, wait until it's as dark as possible. Then go and turn on one light at a time, and one room at a time, to identify any areas that could use more illumination. Change out old bulbs with non-glare 100 W versions (or greater). You can use incandescent bulbs or fluorescent equivalents. Install extra lights where needed.

Here are a few areas where additional lighting might make sense:

- Night lights placed appropriately throughout the house
- LED lighting strips inside and under cabinets
- Lights along staircases
- Lights along floorboards
- Outdoor motion detector lights

Before you permanently install new lighting fixtures, have your loved one tell you which lights they deem too bright or too close. Always be sure to angle lights away so they won't be shining in an elderly person's face.

In general, more illumination is better, but getting lighting right in a home is always a balancing act, especially for macular degeneration patients. You don't want to give them too much of a good thing by creating glare.

I've Fallen, Please Help!

At the time I'm writing this, the installation of a medical alert system comes to around $20 per month. That is such a small price to pay for peace of mind. These packages include buttons that come in the form of a necklace or bracelet. My mom opted for the bracelet because it's less conspicuous and doesn't tangle like a necklace would, especially when cooking.

I would encourage you to get one of these systems and teach your elder to wear the device at all times – even (or especially) when showering or bathing. Not only are the devices fully waterproof and able to dry quickly, but most accidents happen in wet zones. That leads to unfortunate situations where elderly people fear getting the unit wet, take it off, and fall… and can't reach the alert system they are supposed to be wearing for that very reason.

In the Kitchen

What should an age- or health-appropriate kitchen look like? If your senior can afford a complete remodel, these are some features that can make a huge difference while aging in place:

- An open floor plan that allows for the use of a wheelchair or walker
- In-cabinet and under-cabinet lighting
- Wall oven upgrades that eliminate the need to bend over
- Touch-only or touch-free faucets (hands with arthritis have a hard time opening and closing tight fixtures)
- Pull-out cabinets for pots and pans
- A smart home environment

If you're on a budget, don't despair. Here are some creative alternatives to a complete kitchen remodel:

- Remove clutter and unused furniture, like extra chairs, that aren't in use to make more room for a wheelchair or walker.
- Keep floors clean and remove any obstacles.
- Add stick-on LED in-cabinet and under-cabinet lighting.
- Buy a large toaster/convection oven that goes on the countertop to eliminate the need to bend over a conventional oven.
- Replace old sticky faucets with new ones that have easy-turn levers.
- Put heavier, bulkier items like pots and pans at waist level while moving lighter items to lower shelves.
- Store small items in plastic bins you can easily pull out.

- Add bright sticky tabs to on and off positions on oven and microwave knobs (ideal for people with macular degeneration and other vision impairments).

- Use small appliances with an audio tone and auto shutoff feature.

- Look at stores like IKEA to find cleverly designed household items and furniture that make life easier.

Just as important as reconfiguring their home is having your elder practice safe behavior in the kitchen:

- Mark purchase dates on food items and check for freshness.

- Keep hazardous cleaning agents in separate storage well away from food items.

- Don't leave knives lying around; store them safely in a drawer or rack.

- Make it a habit to turn on lights for cooking, even during the day.

- Always set a timer when cooking.

Handrails Galore

Handrails might not look sexy, but they add a lot to the safety of a home for your senior. Wherever you can install them you should. They are fairly inexpensive and easy to put in place.

Handrails come in a variety of different materials: wood, plastic, and brushed aluminum to name just a few. The wooden varieties look less clinical if you care about aesthetics. It could happen that your senior lives in a place where handrails are not a possibility (for instance, if the landlord won't allow them), or they may be resistant to placing them throughout the house. If that's the case, try to at least place them in the bathroom next to the toilet, shower, and tub. It may also be helpful to place them along the walls on the way from the bed to the bathroom.

Along the same lines, you'll definitely want to ensure your senior has railings on both sides of any interior or exterior staircases.

In the Bathroom

There is plenty you can do to make bathrooms safer for your elderly loved one:

- Add a toilet seat riser.

- Clearly mark *hot* and *cold* on faucets.

- Turn temperatures down on the water heater (around 120° is sufficient).

- Add a sturdy bathroom chair for the shower.

- Install a bathtub lift.

- Make sure the bathroom lock can be opened from the outside if needed.

- Add non-skid mats and flooring.

- Add stable and secure grab bars.

Preventing Uninvited Access to the Home

Elderly people are more vulnerable in their homes and naturally are concerned about intruders and break-ins. You can do your part to make them feel safe by identifying any weaknesses of their home, rectifying any problems, and investing in appropriate security systems.

- Secure the property with an alarm system.

- If possible, install security cameras at entry points to the home.

- Remove chain or keys that lock doors from the inside (these can be difficult for elderly people, and if they panic in an emergency they may not be able to open the door to let responders inside).

- Install lever deadbolts on main entrances (these are easier to feel in the dark).

- Install a peephole (a.k.a. peekaboo) on the front door.
- Secure patio doors.
- Secure basement doors.
- Secure garage doors.

Remember how your parents told you not to go with anyone offering you a cookie when you were a child? You need to train your aging parent not to trust anyone they don't know when answering the front door. Sadly, older people can be targets for fraud, scams, and even violent crimes. Make sure your senior knows and understands the lurking dangers. Be proactive about educating them when it comes to the most common scams, along with ways to identify an imposter.

Drug Safety

Seniors can sometimes mistake medications or take the wrong dosages. You can help them be safer by following these steps:

- Have medication dispensed in a convenient dispenser.
- Review medicines frequently with your loved one's doctor or pharmacist, especially when a new medication has been prescribed.
- Fully understand their side effects and potentially negative drug interactions.
- Make sure all medication is clearly labeled and properly stored.
- Make sure your elder has enough light to read the labels so they can take the right medicines and the correct dose.
- Dispose of any older unused medicines.
- Make sure they know not to borrow prescription drugs from others.
- Make sure your elder can't mix drugs and alcohol.
- Check with your loved one's doctor or pharmacist before mixing non-prescription drugs with prescription medications.

General Home Safety

Fires and other emergencies are especially dangerous for older people. Here are some ways to protect them:

- Advise your elder to never smoke alone, when in bed, or on the sofa.

- Install smoke and carbon monoxide detectors on every floor, and keep a fire extinguisher handy.

- Make sure the electrical system and electronics (wiring, fans, air conditioner, heaters, etc.) are all functioning properly.

- Have easily accessible phones in all rooms.

Getting Smart with Smart Home Technology Solutions

Wouldn't it be nice if your older family member was technologically savvy enough to operate every modern gadget without fail and had a smart home fully adapted to senior living? It sure would be. Unfortunately, in all likelihood it's exactly the opposite. It's understandable if installing smart home devices might be the last thing on your mind after getting a hundred calls from your mother asking for help with her computer. But that doesn't mean it's not a good idea.

> *While it's true my parents never even owned a computer or knew how to operate a cell phone, they did benefit from my knowledge on which devices would be helpful to them. Today my mother is a proud owner of an "Alexa" and it amazes me how quickly she learned to make full use of her new friend's capabilities. I guess it's never too late to teach someone a new trick.*

To ignore the benefits of smart home technology would be a huge mistake. As people age, their eyesight and hearing deteriorate, while at the same time they lose dexterity and their mobility can be impaired. So, even if they have been keeping up with technology, the chances are good that as they get older using something as simple as a TV remote control can begin to present a challenge. That's where integrated, voice-activated smart home solutions come in.

Why Smart Home Technology?

Smart home tech can make life easier for everyone, young or old, but it has some very specific benefits for elderly people living at home. They can use web-connected devices to make their home more comfortable, get easier access to entertainment, and (most importantly) increase their safety. And of course, smart home devices have the added advantages of being reasonably affordable and easy to set up. In most cases you can get started with just a mobile phone and an internet connection.

There is little doubt smart home devices have value to your loved one, and to you as a care organizer. With permission, you can use them to check in on your senior and enjoy the peace of mind that comes with knowing they are safe in their home.

Before making any modifications or upgrades, though, you should observe your senior to figure out where those daily risks and struggles lie. Once you know what kind of help they could use, you might consider these four smart home solutions as a starting point:

Alarm Systems

Smart alarm systems allow you to arm and disarm your security from anywhere – you can turn them on and off while you're out and about, when you're traveling, or even from your own bed. Many also incorporate two-way technology that allows you to talk to a live person if you have a medical emergency or fear you may have an intruder. The operator can call the authorities, or medical care providers, as needed. Some services also provide smart smoke detectors that send an alert straight to the company if they sense a fire. That can cut down on the emergency response time.

Security Cameras and Doorbells

Security cameras on your loved one's doors, along with a video door-bell that allows them to see who is there before opening, can be invaluable. No one wants their elderly parents letting strangers into the home. These can also be used by care organizers to monitor the house as needed.

Wearable Devices

Wearable health monitoring devices can help care organizers keep tabs on elderly loved ones and alert paramedics in the event of an emergency. They can also help with things like glucose monitoring and blood pressure readings that can be shared with physicians during scheduled visits. Other technology to keep your elderly loved one safe includes wearable fall alert devices and medical alert buttons that let them reach operators even if they can't get to a phone.

> Even if your loved one isn't tech savvy, smart home devices can simplify their life...and yours.

Home Assistant Devices

Whether you prefer Alexa, Google Home, or some other device, these digital assistants can do everything from adding items to your grocery list to remembering dates, telling you about the weather, or operating other connected systems like the home's lights, thermostat, or cleaning appliances.

"Pukas" is a Hawaiian word for small holes. Regardless of how much help you have organized for your aging parent, there will always be pukas in their day when you wish you could be there but can't.

Filling the Pukas
Creating a Support Network

E ven when you do everything you can hiring help or situating your loved one in a great age-appropriate facility, you'll probably find it isn't enough. What you need, but can't usually get, is someone who looks at the big picture to take your place when you can't be there. In theory you could hire a case manager to look after your aging parent, but a professional may charge $100 an hour or more to manage an older person. And even if cost isn't a barrier, in many rural communities it can be very difficult to find someone qualified to help.

And besides, you don't necessarily need a team of specialists. It's often the little things, like not being able to open a can of tomatoes, that cause headaches for older people and make them feel particularly inept and helpless. Rather than ask for assistance, they will try to manage frustrating tasks on their own until they become miserable enough to give up. Knowing they can't perform simple chores any longer becomes very depressing.

My mother would often drop the tiny batteries that went into her hear-ing aid on the floor, and then wouldn't be able to find them or pick them up. Of course, she could always use a new battery, but that wasn't the point. The real issue was that the small changes life presented her didn't just happen once. They came up again and again. With time she started to become very upset and frustrated with herself. Tasks that were easy for a younger and more able person became more and more insurmountable for her. She needed someone she could lean on for assistance, and the occasional shoulder to cry on.

Even if you hire a cleaner, a gardener, a handyman, and a nurse, chances are there will be small gaps – little pukas – where your loved one still needs a helping hand on occasion. It makes sense to get them the assistance they need within the community. In some neighbor-hoods there are groups of teenagers or retirees who will gladly volun-teer. Finding these kinds of resources made a huge difference for me as a care organizer.

I cannot stress enough how important it is to start building a net-work of people around your senior. These can be neighbors, friends, acquaintances, or even volunteers from a reputable agency. They might come from a community service for seniors, or be someone who is re-ferred by a self-help group. It can be someone you know personally, or someone you don't know at all. According to the Family Caregiver Alliance (visit **caregiver.org**) more than 44 million Americans aged 18 and over provide unpaid assistance and support to older people and adults with disabilities in their community. Help is out there if you go looking for it.

It is essential you have someone to look after your aging family mem-ber on a regular basis while you are back at home living your life. You need people to pop in once in a while to bring over some soup or provide a word of encouragement. Without having that someone in place, you will be in constant agony and worry. You probably won't be able to relax.

I hated knowing there were these little holes in my mom's life when

I couldn't be around. Living with those pukas was heartbreaking and frustrating... until I found a fix.

One of the most important and valuable people in my mother's life is a volunteer from a local senior-focused organization. She was a total stranger when she was first introduced to us, and neither I nor my mother thought the two of them would grow so close. In fact, both of us were hesitant to accept the help in the beginning. Now, Mom adores her volunteer and says she is her "angel." Wouldn't it be nice if you had an angel for your loved one, too?

Things started when I signed my mom up for 24/7 emergency alert service. While visiting the company I saw a brochure lying around in which volunteers were being recruited to help fragile seniors through a local non-profit. I knew I couldn't possibly volunteer myself, being situated thousands of miles away, but figured it couldn't hurt to call the organization to find out more about the program. Sure enough they had just recruited someone new – a woman in her 60s was waiting to be assigned to a senior household. We made an appointment with the program coordinator, who arranged a meeting with my mother to see if her personality would be a good match for the volunteer.

The social companionship program works like this: the volunteer would spend two hours per week with their assigned elder. The purpose was to get seniors out of the home for a change of scenery, and to provide opportunities for socialization to curb isolation. The senior could pick an activity, or the volunteer could suggest one. In lieu of compensation, we paid the volunteer for any expenses incurred during the outing.

My mom's favorite pastime was kaffeeklatsch, coffee and cake. So, the ladies would go out to the coffeeshop and sit and chat. When my mother needed to go to the doctor, Mrs. G (I want to omit her full name to protect her privacy) would accompany her. Mrs. G has been a great influence on my mom. When I tried to convince my mother she needed a walker, she wouldn't listen to me. But, it turned out she would listen to her "angel" instead. In case you're wondering, it didn't hurt my feelings at all. Well, maybe just a little.

It has been amazing to watch how quickly the two have bonded with each other. When I have to fly back home to Hawaii, I have complete con-

fidence and peace of mind knowing there is someone we can both count on. Today, Mrs. G is more than a volunteer to us. She has become a part of our small family.

One reason things work out so well is that we all stick very strictly to the rules. We don't ever ask our volunteer to go over her allotted time unless there is something (like a concert or special event) that Mrs. G also wants to be a part of. We always cover her expenses. And needless to say, the occasional bottle of bubbly goes a long way toward expressing our appreciation.

In addition to this companion, I've also groomed a network of people in the neighborhood, and even rounded up some of my old friends, who are able to help out on occasion.

Here is another example of engaging the community in a creative way.

When winter came, my mother became very stressed about shoveling the snow. She had arthritis and was afraid of slipping and falling on the ice. I told her we would hire a snow removal service and thought "problem solved." It turned out the neighbor kids got upset when we had the white fluffy stuff taken away. They had waited so long for it to snow, and when it finally did we had it removed. Their hearts had been set on building a ramp for sledding and we had unknowingly ruined their plans.

Thankfully we got another dump of snow a week later and by then I'd canceled the removal service. This time the kids lined up with their shovels and got to take away all the fluffy powder they needed for their projects. With our donation into their piggy bank account, they bought a new sled and were super stoked to help out. A win-win for everyone!

For some, it might feel awkward to reach out to neighbors and friends at first. If that's you, my advice is to just get over it. You don't want to limit yourself to having just one or two individuals for support. The more the merrier. Once you build your network and find your angel, you need to collect and distribute contact information – including *your* contact information – among the main players in case of an emergency. Here in Hawaii we call this kind of arrangement "the coconut wireless" and it works great. Don't forget to make sure everyone on your list knows you have prepared a bag for the hospital for your loved one, along with where to find it.

There is no need to give every person who might be looking in on your elder a key to the house so long as you're confident someone close by has access to your senior's home. It doesn't hurt to spell out in some detail who is in charge of which tasks, and who can be contacted for backup. When people see you are organized and on top of things they will be more willing to jump in when your loved one needs assistance.

Be sure to spread out the tasks. If you are always asking the same person for assistance that can become an issue in itself. Friends and neighbors might be less inclined to offer a helping hand if you make it a habit to call on them without showing gratitude or reciprocating. Also remember that you can still be a good neighbor even if you live thousands of miles away from your senior, as I do. Here's a hint: *Amazon delivers almost everywhere.*

Just as it was when you were looking for a health care provider or elder care lawyer, you need to do your diligence and learn to spot red flags when building this kind of informal network. However, so long as you have vetted the potential support provider thoroughly and feel 100% confident in that person, things should work out just fine.

Here Are Some Tips on Making a Safe Decision

- Only use reputable agencies for your search.
- Carefully read volunteer profiles.
- See what others have to say about a candidate.
- Always verify phone and email information.
- Try to interview in person, or if that is not possible, via video chat.
- Ask yourself: does the person appear professional, calm, and supportive?
- Find out how much experience the candidate has with seniors.
- What age group have they cared for?
- Is the candidate trained in CPR and first aid?
- Has the person taken any classes in geriatric care?
- Is the person able and willing to lift heavy objects?
- Does the candidate speak your loved one's language?
- Has the person handled an emergency, and if so what happened?
- How would the candidate handle a difficult situation?
- Are there responsibilities this person would rather not take on?
- Check references and contact previous employers.
- Check social media sites for relevant public information.
- Do a background check to reveal any criminal record or driving history.

- Only share your own contact information if you
  feel comfortable with the candidate.

You will want to tailor your questions to your specific situation. Don't let your guard down too early, and don't ever tolerate someone your elder doesn't like or is fearful of. Trust your instincts and theirs.

A Word of Caution

While there are many online resources for finding the kinds of little helpers you need, I feel your best and safest bet is word-of-mouth within your own personal network. If you are going to search the internet, the two web portals I would trust are the Volunteers of America at **voa.org** and the AARP, which can be accessed at **aarp.org**.

Without being overly paranoid or overbearing, once you have engaged a helper it is a good idea to stay involved to prevent any over-stepping on the part of assistants, caregivers, and volunteers. Check in during times when things go smoothly to keep them honest. Be doubly careful if your elder is still in charge of their money. Black sheep (i.e., fraudsters) can lurk, even among family members, and those who seem at first to be angels may suddenly walk away with the family jewels.

Should you have any doubts or hesitation about engaging a volunteer, or should you need additional assistance in managing your loved one's care, consider hiring a professional seniors advocate. This person will be able to guide you through the myriad options in front of you.

Managing the people who care for your loved one is an art and a skill. It's important to have the right instructions and protocols in place. A few random checks will keep them honest and reduce your sense of worry.

Silent Monitoring

Performing Quality Control of Service Providers

Maybe you have siblings or other family members who are sharing some of the responsibilities of care organization with you. Or, maybe you are like me and have to go it alone and negotiate the world of senior care by yourself. In either case, it's important that everyone is on the same page and communicates clearly. However, it's usually best if one spokesperson is assigned to the task of coordinating and handling caregiving services and keeping others in the loop. That's especially true in large families where conflict could easily arise.

If that job falls on you, know that maintaining good communication with home health aides will be a major part of supporting your parent. Just be prepared for the occasional breakdown of communication between one party and another. That's quite normal. Culture or values might differ, and can often be the underlying reason for disputes. A family member might badmouth the caregiver, or vice versa, and the next thing you know people are at each other's throats.

To Set the Stage for a Positive Relationship, You Need to Agree on A Few Things

First and foremost, everyone needs to have trust and respect for one another. Family members need to be in agreement with each other, and if they aren't they should avoid infighting as much as possible. If there is a great deal of arguing between individual family members it might make sense to engage a mediator to simply cool frayed nerves by identifying sources of friction. These might include unrealistic expectations or nonconstructive criticisms of caregivers and each other.

Hired caregivers in particular will often find themselves caught in family feuds. This is not only unfair to them, but it can also be damaging for the person who is dependent on their benevolent actions and care. For the most part, professional caregivers perform their jobs out of a sense of purpose and conviction. They aren't just in it for the money. As a matter fact, caregiving jobs are not very well paid considering how hard the assignments can be, not to mention the grueling working hours associated with these physically demanding and emotionally draining jobs.

I find it remarkable what these people do. It really isn't the care giver's fault if they receive insufficient training or find themselves doing the job of two on their own. Yet they continue to care for others while receiving little pay or praise. Make no mistake: these jobs are tough, and it's no wonder turnover rates in the industry are extremely high.

Of course, the company providing your home health aides will do anything to get your business. They won't tell you they are running a lean ship, that they underpay their staff, or any of their management problems. Their goal is to sign another contract. It should be *your* goal to find out everything you can about their reputation before you sign your name on the dotted line. Even then, only time will tell whether or not you and your loved one will be satisfied with their service. Just be prepared for the fact that everything might not turn out exactly as promised, or as you had hoped. You'll have to learn the difference between issues that are minor and forgivable and those that are unacceptable.

One of the duties of our home health aide was to administer medication three times per day. Easy, right? It had been my understanding that the administration of medication meant the nurse would give my mother each dosage and watch her take it. It turned out this was not the case. Instead, the nurse would come during the morning hours and prepare the medication by distributing it into a pill dispenser. Then, late in the afternoon a different nurse would check the pill container to see if it was empty.

You might think: "That sounds about right." Not quite. One day I realized something was amiss when I noticed a bunch of pills on the floor. When I asked my mother whether she was aware there was medication lying around her answer was "no." Upon further questioning I discovered that all the staff did was check the pillbox, sign a daily register, and then leave.

In my opinion the system they had in place was flawed. Not only should the staff have checked Mom's pill dispenser, but also the surrounding areas such as countertops and floors. When someone my mother's age, with failing vision, hearing impairments, and a lack of dexterity drops a pill by accident, they wouldn't necessarily notice it.

Luckily, in my mother's case skipping a dose wasn't critical. But what if it was? It's crucial that everything be done correctly. Mistakes like that shouldn't have been happening.

I can't stress enough how important it is for you to fully understand the processes and procedures used by the personnel and services you choose. Pay attention and voice any concerns early on. Have someone you trust do random checks for you if you cannot do them yourself.

You have no influence over the caregivers' working agreements or shift rotations. However, you *can* do your part by providing a clean and well-organized space so they can do their jobs properly. For example, don't expect the caregiver to be a maid if they have not been specifically hired for that task. It's important to communicate early on what you expect of the person and service. Make sure every aide is equally informed and be prepared to spell out their tasks, or any important details, more than once as staff members may change frequently.

I had wondered why home health staff were always rotating, so one day I asked. I was given two reasons. The first was that management didn't want staff to get too close and attached to any particular patient to reduce the emotional burden if that person passed away. The second was to avoid any potential abuse from either side.

From one nurse I learned that a patient had frequently used abusive language whenever she bathed them. She was so upset about it she nearly quit. By rotating caregivers the company avoided placing this burden directly on one person. I also witnessed a nurse trying to manipulate my father and caught her red-handed when she was coaxing him to sign an invoice to be submitted to his insurance company for services that were never rendered. Imagine what she might have tried if she were caring for my parents regularly!

You shouldn't forget to stay vigilant and watch for any signs of elder abuse and neglect. You should also look for evidence your elder might be forgetting his or her manners, whatever the reason. It's hard to have your finger on the pulse of a situation when you aren't present, but if you are informed of the declining conditions – or suspect financial, emotional, or physical abuse – don't hesitate to get help. You can reach out to the long-term care ombudsman or Adult Protective Services (APS) office in your area.

Most states have an agency that deals specifically with elder abuse and fraud. You can find an APS map at **http://www.napsa-now.org/ get-help/help-in-your-area/**. It even has an area designed to provide easy-to-access information on reporting suspected abuse nationwide.

Elder abuse is unfortunately all too common, but hopefully you won't ever have to face those kinds of suspicions. If you follow the advice in this chapter and the next one, you should be able to enjoy the peace of mind that comes with knowing your loved one is in a safe and supportive environment.

Besides, if you show home health aides respect and acknowledge the good work they do, they will generally respond in kind. Don't be afraid to say "*thank you*" or send them small gifts as tokens of your appreciation when you observe them making an effort to provide great care. Showing your gratitude won't hurt. In fact, it benefits everyone.

Don't rely on the internet, fancy advertisements, slick certifications, or a sales-person's sweet talk when selecting a senior home. It's much better to show up un-announced at your top choices and take a good look around. I call it becoming a "mystery shopper."

The Mystery Shopper

From Your First Impression to Your Final Pick

I f aging in place won't work for your loved one, you may have to find a nursing home. You will certainly be able to conduct a lot of preliminary research online, but to really narrow down your choices you will need to see the best options in person.

Do you know the weird feeling you get when you walk into a store you haven't visited before? That slight uneasiness caused by not know-ing what to expect, or wondering whether the sales staff is going to be jumping at you or leaving you alone? That's exactly the same feeling you get when you set foot into a nursing home for the first time. You are either immediately intercepted by some eager employee, or find yourself wandering around the facility undisturbed without being able to locate anyone to talk to when you have questions. Neither is ideal.

Wouldn't it be nice if you were to come across a friendly home administrator who would greet you, show you around without any pressurized sales talk, and give you a detailed description of the facility? Imagine having them introduce you to some of the lead nursing staff and allow you to look around on your own. What would it be like if you could get a sense for the place without the use of sneaky sales tactics or attempts to shmooze and upsell you? Going even further, think about what it would be like if your loved one could be offered a trial stay for a couple of weeks. I can almost see you shaking your head in disbelief, but believe me these places do exist.

Identifying the right senior facility shouldn't be anxiety provoking. It should be fun and rewarding, which it is when you find the right option. When you discover the ultimate digs for your loved one it's something you can feel really good about, especially if you visited multiple times after diligently researching your choices and carefully evaluating each one. You can find a place your parent will want to call "home."

Of course, the other side of the coin also applies. It can be a huge hassle – and a costly mistake – if your elder doesn't like the facility you choose. Moving is very stressful at any age, but much more so for an older person. For that reason your senior's new living quarters need to pass your most important tests, and theirs.

With so much on the line, it's time to click your heels and get ready for some serious undercover investigation work.

First, I want you to go and visit the places closest to the location your loved one would like to live in. You can always expand your search to include facilities farther away, if needed. While it's good to stay in the neighborhood your elder wants to live in, you don't want to limit yourself so strictly when a better home or facility could be waiting in the next town over.

The more you can find out about a senior care facility and its services the better. Visit any home you are considering at least three times, with each visit coming at a different time of day. By doing so you will be able to see different sets of staff, and also observe residents in different settings. It's impossible to take everything in when visiting once. And when you do stop by, don't just look around. Talk to residents and staff and, if it's allowed, take some pictures. That way you will be able to remember more of the details later. Just be sure you respect the privacy of the residents when snapping photographs.

My mystery shopping experiments began long before I had even talked to my parents about the idea of a nursing home. At that time there was no immediate need for them to move, and I had no reason for alarm. I simply wanted to get a feel for what was out there – a little head start on what I suspected might be a long process.

I tried visiting first at lunchtime, then during scheduled activities, and later during the "quiet hours" so I could observe the residents and staff during peak hours and off hours. During those outings I encountered everything from screaming matches between staff members to unkempt patients being wheeled off and left to themselves in corners. I also saw residents being hugged lovingly by genuinely caring personnel.

In other words, I saw the good and the bad. And, even as upsetting as some of it was, in the end I was really glad I made the effort. It allowed me to weed out some of the options and only show my parents the kinds of places I would seriously entertain. I didn't want them to be confronted by, and burdened with, some of the ugly realities I wanted to keep them away from.

During your visits, use all your senses. Sharpen your ears, your eyes, and even your nose. What impression do you get from the residents? Do they appear open and content, agile, and well groomed? Are they dressed in clean clothes? Or do they seem apathetic, soiled, intimidated, and resigned? Do the common areas and apartment rooms smell clean, or do you detect human waste? Keep in mind that strong incense or air fresheners indicate the latter. Listen to the tone of voice personnel use when they interact with patients. What sort of style does the staff use with slow patients? Do caregivers seem understanding, kind, or frustrated and impatient?

> It pays to pay attention to details.

Although you want to see an "unscripted" version of the nursing home, you should also ask lots of questions. Talk to as many people as possible, starting in the parking lot and continuing all the way into the main common areas. Find out what a typical day is like in the home or facility.

Whenever I saw someone who seemed like they were either coming or going at the nursing homes I visited, I approached them. It didn't matter whether they were residents, visitors, relatives, cleaning personnel, nursing staff, or even drivers. It was easy and no one ever turned me away.

My script went like this: "Excuse me, do you have a minute? My name is Petra, and I'm in the process of deciding a nursing home for my mom.

Would you mind if I asked you a few questions? Is it your parent who is living here? Is she satisfied and glad to be living here, and are you too? What can you tell me about the place? What does a normal day look like? Do you have any complaints or reasons to be unhappy with your choice? How are the personnel treating the residents? Is the staff making sure your loved one comes to meals? If you could change something, what would it be? Is the management responsive to any complaints and suggestions?"

My script for engaging with personnel would be very similar. I would ask questions like: "I see you are working here. Since when, if I may ask? What do you do? Do you like working here? How would you describe the working environment?"

How many of your questions will be answered will depend a great deal on how much time the person has and how talkative they are. You certainly don't want to push too hard, and you should be respectful of other people's time.

It was amazing the kind of responses and feedback I got. People were really open to sharing their experiences. I think it's because so many others had been there and done that. They knew how hard it could be, and exactly what I was going through. The places I left on my list had a healthy mix of positive and negative responses. However, the negative responses were regarding issues that didn't matter much to my mother and me.

Of course, speaking only to people you run into randomly isn't going to be sufficient to help you complete your research. You will also want to speak to someone in home administration and/or management. For that step, you may need to schedule an appointment. When the time comes, visit prepared so you don't waste your time (or theirs).

As you gather information on potential nursing homes you should put it into a spreadsheet. Not only is it easy to forget data that is improperly recorded, but you might want to be able to compare and evaluate your findings together with your elder at some point. Luckily, I have prepared exactly such a spreadsheet for you. You can download the file to your computer from **theeldercareplaybook.com** and customize it to reflect your own situation and results. You can also use the same template to research adult day care centers, and parts of it are applicable when you review home health aide providers. After all, the concerns and questions are very similar.

RESEARCHING FACILITIES   last updated:

NAME AND LOCATION OF FACILITY

BRIEF SUMMARY OF YOUR FIRST IMPRESSION

GENERAL	ANSWER
What is the location and surrounding like?	
Do they offer printed information voluntarily or did you have to ask?	
Can the interested patient meet with you for a preliminary discussion?	
Can terminally ill patients live there until the end?	
Do you house patients with Alzheimers/Dementia?	
Notes:	

BUILDING / FACILITY / SURROUNDINGS	ANSWER
Is the facility certified to operate in the state?	
Where is it located? (City proper or countryside?)	
Is the neighborhood quiet or noisy? Vibrant or serene? Other?	
How close to public transport?	
What type of shops are nearby?	
Close to cultural events or programs?	
Is there ample visitors parking?	
How many handicap parking stalls?	
Is this the only property or is it part of a company with multiple houses?*	
Did you see the state's most recent inspection report? (Public information)	

*often there are more options available to residents.

BUILDING / FACILITY / SURROUNDINGS   ANSWER

If any, how many and what type of complaints have been filed against the property in the last 2 years?

How many rooms/residents does the facility have?

How many elevators does it have?

Is the facility oversee-able?

Are the common areas easily accessible and easy to find?

Are all areas well lit?

Are all areas wheelchair accessible and barrier free?

Does it have a wheelchair accessible garden?

Is there an area to park a walker?

What are the amenities? (TV rooms, Fitness, Library, Beauty Parlor, etc.)

Is the building well maintained, clean and secure?

Does it have a chapel?

Does it have rooms for rent for guests or visiting relatives?

Is there a space one can rent for a private party?

Is the atmosphere friendly, homey, or sterile? (Describe)

Is there a special, secluded wing for patients with Alzheimers/Dementia?

How well is the medical and rehab therapy area equipped?

What is the dining area like?

Is there a convenience store or station for visitors?

Are pets allowed?

Are quiet times or visitation hours strictly enforced?

BUILDING / FACILITY / SURROUNDINGS   ANSWER

Can the rooms be locked?

Are the residents free to come and go?

Is there a curfew at night time?

Notes:

INDIVIDUAL ROOMS / COMMON AREAS   ANSWER

Are there rooms for single occupancy?

Are there rooms for double occupancy?

Do rooms have private bathrooms with walk-in showers?

Are the rooms adequate in size?

What are the rooms like, are they modern and well kept?

What are the bathrooms like?

Are there gender specific bathrooms?

Is there an emergency call system in the living as well as bathroom area?

Are there handrails and a chair for the shower in the bathroom?

Are there rooms for single occupancy?

Are there rooms for double occupancy?

Do rooms have private bathrooms with walk-in showers?

Are the rooms adequate in size?

What are the rooms like, are they modern and well kept?

INDIVIDUAL ROOMS / COMMON AREAS	ANSWER

What are the bathrooms like?

Are there gender specific bathrooms?

Is there an emergency call system in the living as well as bathroom area?

Are there handrails and a chair for the shower in the bathroom?

Are the rooms sufficiently furnished?

Are the rooms bright, friendly and cozy?

Can the rooms be furnished or decorated with personal belongings?

Who is the Telephone, TV, Internet/WIFI provider?

What is the additional cost for Phone, TV, etc., if any?

Do I get a new phone # or can I port my number?

Do the rooms have a balcony or terrace?

Is there enough space for storage?

Is there a safe to store valuables?

Is there enough space in double rooms for privacy?

Are the common areas nicely decorated?

Is there a lounge?

Is there a TV room?

Is there a library?

What is the common dining area like?

Is the seating comfortable?

Are there lockers for safe keep of personal items during activities?

INDIVIDUAL ROOMS / COMMON AREAS   ANSWER

Notes:

NURSING STAFF   ANSWER

Is the ratio of nursing staff to size of facility adequate?

Is the facility sufficiently staffed during day and night times?

How about on weekends?

Is the reception area staffed at all times?

Would you describe the staff as friendly, caring and respectful of the residents?

Does the staff take time for the residents or do they seem stressed?

Does the staff help with eating if needed?

Or do patients have to manage on their own?

How many registered nurses are on staff at any given time?

What is the ratio between qualified and unqualified nursing staff?

How much ongoing training does the staff receive and in what intervals?

How many nurses for special cases (dementia, diabetes, stroke, cancer)?

Does the staff appear friendly, caring and compassionate with residents?

Does the staff appear to be stressed and overworked?

Does the staff appear to be content and cheerful?

NURSING STAFF	ANSWER

Notes:

ASSISTANCE AND MEDICAL CARE	ANSWER

Do the residents have a say in how much care they will receive?

Will you provide a care plan?

Can the resident decide when they want to be bathed?

Can the resident choose the nurse?

Is there a medical doctor on the premises?

Can I keep my doctors and have them do house visits?

How well does the facility cooperate with my own doctors?

Do you schedule doctor's visits and other appointments?

Will medical procedures or therapies be discussed with the patient?

Can I choose my own therapist, or do I have to use intern?

Do you offer Music or Art Therapy?

What social services do you offer?

Do you help with filling out applications (such as reimbursements)?

Do you offer support to and from doctors's visits?

Do you use restraints for patients who wander or alternative methods?

ASSISTANCE AND MEDICAL CARE	ANSWER
Do you store and administer medications for residents?	
Do you use medications to control behavior or alternative methods?	
Do you provide transportation to and from doctor's appointments?	
How qualified is the night staff and how many nurses are there for the night shift?	
Do you offer massages and other alternative methods to treating pain?	
Do you provide palliative care?	
Do you provide hospice care?	
Are you part of a volunteer companionship network?	
Notes:	

MEALS AND BEVERAGES	ANSWER
Are the meals prepared fresh every day?	
Are they cooked in house or delivered?	
Are meals balanced, healthy and nutritious?	
Can I eat in my room and also in the dining room?	
Are visitors allowed in the dining room?	
Is seating assigned?	
How many meals per day?	
Is there a meal plan?	
Can I choose my meal?	

MEALS AND BEVERAGES — ANSWER

Can I choose my meal?

Can I choose when I want to eat?

Can I get food and beverages between scheduled meals?

Do you offer special diets?

Do you pay attention to food allergies?

Would you respect personal dietary preferences?

Are beverages included in the monthly fee?

Do you offer alcoholic beverages?

Do you offer snacks?

Do offer coffee and cake in the afternoon?

Do you have a refrigerator one can use?

Do you assist with food intake?

Can I come to test the food?

Notes:

CLEANLINESS AND HYGIENE — ANSWER

Does the facility look and smell clean?

How often are the rooms being cleaned?

Do you clean personal items if needed?

Does cleaning crew respect patients' quiet times?

Can I use my own bedsheets and towels?

CLEANLINESS AND HYGIENE   ANSWER

How often is laundry being done?

Does the laundry service include ironing and mending?

Are cleaning and laundry services included
in the price?

How often do you check and clean patients
with incontinence?

How often to patients get bathed or showered?

I like to take a bath once a month, do you have
a deep bathtub?

Notes:

ACTIVITIES   ANSWER

Do you offer a variety of musical, cultural, spiritual and
social activities? Singing, dancing, games, reading,
mobility training, cognitive training, walks, painting,
music, crafts, church, movies, theatre, concerts, zoo,
etc.

Do you offer special activities for patients with
dementia, physical or vision impairment?

Do you offer activities specifically geared for men or
women?

How do you organize activities to match the resident's
preferences?

How often do you offer activities?

How do you promote activity participation?

When do you have social hours or visitation hours?

Can Children visit?

ACTIVITIES   ANSWER

What about pets visiting?

Do you organize activities or take residents to events
outside the home?

Do you provide transportation?

What if the resident wants to leave early or
doesn't feel good?

Notes:

ACCOUNTABILITY & ADMINISTRATION   ANSWER

Do you have a complaint manager?

What are the opening hours to speak to management?

How do you track, record & measure a resident's
well-being?

Do you share the well-being assessment report?

How do you keep families informed?

Do you offer safe keeping for valuables?

Do you safe keep allowances and offer teller services?

Who deals with Medicare/Medicaid, or supplemental
insurance?

How does billing and payment work? EFT?

Do you offer banking services?

Will I have a cash account for an allowance?

Who helps with administration in case of
a hospital stay?

ACCOUNTABILITY & ADMINISTRATION   ANSWER

Notes:

COSTS & CONTRACT   ANSWER

Are the contract details easy to understand?

Is it transparent what is included in the monthly cost?

Are the costs and services clearly itemized
in the contract?

How much does it cost per month?

What is my out-of-pocket monthly cost?

What percentage will be paid by Medicare/
Medicaid?

What are my options to receive financial aid?

Are the prices for additional services adequate?

For how long is the contract?

What is the cancellation policy?

Under what circumstances can the nursing home
terminate the contract?

How long before the room has to be vacated
upon death?

Do you offer a trial stay?

Is there a registration period?

How long is the waiting period?

COSTS & CONTRACT	ANSWER
Notes:	

To get more information, find out from neighbors, friends, and even public sources (like news articles or blog posts) what reputation the senior facility has. It's good to have as many points of information as you can, but don't simply accept what others are saying. This is true whether you're reading something online or hearing it in person. Whether a senior home is "good" or "bad" is an individual subjective perception. Some people like a multitude of activities, while others may pay more attention to food or modern amenities. Certain individuals will want a luxurious place to live while others might wish for a modest home under Christian management. Only you know what's important to your loved one, so let that be your guide.

This is a long list of questions. And I don't doubt you could think of even more to ask. Don't expect you will collect an answer for every little detail; turning this into a rigorous exam isn't the point of this exercise. What I would like you to walk away with is the importance of getting a real sense for the nursing homes you visit, and for you to bring yourself a step closer to what you and your loved one are looking for. What conclusions can you draw after a week, or month, of ongoing research?

Checking out different nursing homes and facilities can be overwhelming. Every person you meet will want you to think their amenities and advantages are the best, even if they aren't relevant to your situation or your senior's preferences. By using the provided checklists, you can stay focused on what matters to you and come away with organized notes you can refer back to later. Those notes will become more and more valuable to you over time, both because your memory might otherwise fade and because you'll develop a better idea of what you need for your loved one.

> *The first time I stepped into a nursing home I was reminded of my own fragile existence, and the possibility that I might end up in one of those places myself. The idea terrified me. Good grief, how could I possibly want this for my parents?*
>
> *As I have already mentioned, most people I spontaneously approached on my own were very open and willing to answer my questions. That wasn't always the case with home administration or management, which surprised me. Some administrators I encountered were not forthcoming at all, and tried to get rid of me as quickly as possible by handing me colorful brochures to read. After being shooed away I had to wonder if they honestly thought I would consider signing my parents up with a facility that wouldn't even extend me the courtesy of showing me around or answering my questions. Then I left.*
>
> *Other administrators tried to coax me with weird persuasive talk. I found that really annoying, too. One line I heard quite often was, "Since you live so far away, wouldn't you like to have the best for your mother?" Having someone nudge at that little voice of inner guilt in my mind made me feel really uncomfortable. Of course I wanted the best for her, but two questions came to mind. First, could they really demonstrate that their facility lived up to the standards? And second, how would they know what was best for my mother? Sorry, but that tactic wasn't going to work for me – I didn't want to be persuaded today only to have my mom be miserable tomorrow.*
>
> *I surprised myself a bit during those visits. I knew I didn't want to walk away disillusioned and exhausted, which would have been easy given that it involved a lot of emotionally challenging work. Instead of letting those things get to me, I simply stayed focused on the big picture and stuck to my mission.*

It is my sincere hope that, equipped with this long laundry list, you're able to narrow your choices down and find a suitable place for your loved one to live. If you remain uncertain, *keep looking!* Unless you are

100% confident that the home is the best fit for your loved one and meets your standards (and theirs), you shouldn't be in a rush to move your elder.

Also remember that you might want to have more than one selection. In fact, you may have a "top choice facility" and another that you keep in the back of your mind (and notes) as "Plan B."

Even if you have done the best you possibly can with your preparations, and have done all of your homework, it's possible you will need to change course at some point. What happens if the facility you have chosen changes management? What if your loved one's needs change? What if your own situation is altered, if you need to consider new locations, or if there are legal and financial challenges to the arrangement from the elder or other family members?

These sorts of possibilities have to be considered, which can add an extra layer of complexity to your planning and evaluation process. Just take things gradually and try to approach the situation with a clear mind.

During moments of frustration – and there will probably be a few – try to remind yourself why you're going through all the time and trouble. When a move into a nursing home has to happen quickly, you don't have the luxury of time to shop around and do in-depth analysis. Your only choice might be to take whichever facility is available at the moment. By researching things ahead of time, you're making it possible to achieve a much better outcome for yourself and your senior.

When dealing with an acute situation, a great deal will be demanded of you. Dropping everything at a moment's notice is hard. Hopefully you have gotten everything in place at this point so you can get to where you are needed most – with your elder.

Tower, We Have an Emergency

Dealing With a Crisis and Making the Move

You never know where you will be when you get the much-dreaded phone call that something bad has happened. You never anticipate the moment when you will have to drop everything and get in a car or hop on a plane. Accidents or unexpected illnesses happen when you least expect them, and you will never really be prepared for your elder to have an emergency. This is the moment where the roles are reversed – you have to give it your best shot and be the parent now. But if you have done your homework, at least you will be able to travel without having to worry too much about paperwork or the legal or financial aspects of the crisis. That gives you the chance to be fully present with your loved one and just focus on what comes next.

For months I had been planning my mother's birthday, along with the trip overseas to see her. Preparations went smoothly and everyone invited had sent in their RSVPs. Even better, my mom had been in really good spirits. She was beyond excited to see her friends and family soon. All that was left to do is get there. The usually grueling 24-plus-hour trip didn't even seem that long because I was looking forward to what would come next.

Touch down. After several long flights I finally arrived at the airport in my hometown. Finally, I heard those comforting words: "Please keep your seatbelts fastened until the pilot has turned off the seatbelt fastened sign. You may now use your electronic devices." I pulled out my mobile phone and switched it on. I wasn't expecting any messages since friends and clients knew I would be away.

Instead, my phone woke to a loud "Bing! Bing!" sound. A single text message scrolled across the screen: "Your mother had a fall yesterday. Her condition is not critical but she's in the hospital having surgery today. Please call this number and proceed immediately to the hospital."

Good grief. In a heartbeat, all the happy excitement about my trip vanished. It was replaced with the worry about how badly my mother was injured, what would be waiting for me when I arrived at the hospital, and what the future might hold. A whirlwind of agonizing thoughts swarmed into my mind.

By the time I reached the clinic my mother was already in recovery. I made it just in time to be there when she opened her eyes. She was pretty beaten up, and the first thing she did when she saw me was mumble something along the lines of "I am so sorry…"

> Being there for your loved one when you are most needed matters.

"Shush, silly, no need to be sorry. You will get back on your feet and will have your party," I reassured her, even though I hadn't yet seen the medical report.

As it turned out, Mom had tried to get up from her La-Z-Boy when the phone rang. But instead of making it to the line as she had thousands of times before, for some bizarre reason she stumbled and fell like a log, landing flat on her face. When she hit the ground she broke her left elbow. Instead of pressing the emergency button to call for immediate help, she slowly crawled toward the phone, got on her knees, and dialed her angel's cell phone number. Mrs. G was already on her way – she was the one who called earlier and found it was odd my mother didn't pick up when she rang. When she arrived she loaded Mom into her car and took her to the nearest hospital, where they prepared her for surgery right away.

It was a bad day for everyone, but in a way we all got lucky. It could've been so much worse.

Did we have her party? You bet we did. Two days after her surgery Mom was released, and a week later we gathered to celebrate her 90th just as planned. Mom might have been badly bruised, but her swollen face was covered in makeup and her arm was placed in a cast. She looked weary but smiled for every picture, looking noticeably grateful to be at the celebration.

When a crisis occurs, you will need to put your life on a temporary hold. You have to be there with all your strength and being, wearing your nurse's hat and staying focused so you can care for your elder until they get better or you have someone to take over for you. It can be difficult to deal with the hiccups of someone else's life when you already have a full plate on your own, but that's just part of this journey. You can't fully prepare for it, but you can put yourself in a position to give your love and attention when they can make all the difference.

No more ifs or buts. Nursing home it is.

No matter how much planning and preparation you do, unexpected emergencies are bound to come up. While some accidents or illnesses can be cured, others might have such dire consequences that the patient has no other choice but to move into a skilled nursing facility.

When the time comes to put your elder's moving plan in motion, all you have to do is stay focused, keep your loved one comfortable, and make the transition to a nursing facility as smooth as possible. The plan you created will have hopefully been shared with other family members. That way you can all use it as an anchor to come back to, and a point of reference for others to take over when you need a break.

As the move unfolds, it can be helpful if you engage your elderly loved one in the preparations to the degree that they are willing or able. You might let them participate in shopping for small furnishings, buying new clothes, or setting aside keepsakes to bring along. Even though their involvement will most likely slow the process down, it's important for them to know they still have a say.

Most nursing homes will provide a list of suggestions about what to pack. How much you bring will depend on how large your elder's room is, how much closet space there is to work with, and whether you are allowed to bring a dresser or bins for additional storage. This will probably be the ultimate downsizing challenge for you and your loved one.

As a general rule, you should only discard items your loved one is ready to part with. That's true even if you can't bring those items along, or think they might be useless (or even plain ol' garbage). Remember you can always set things aside and make a dump run later, after the dust settles. At the same time, you should also not be tempted to give in to demands of bringing too many things into a new place.

A nursing home is not a storage facility. If you come to an impasse with your elder about their "precious" possessions, you might want to seek advice from a consultant who can work with you to pare down to the essentials (along with a few items that are near and dear to their heart). If that isn't an option and you can't reason with your senior, designate a corner or box for *things to perhaps move later.* You can tell them that they need to prioritize and only gather possessions that are critical, for now, and suggest that once those items have found their place in the room you can bring the rest.

Beyond knowing which possessions should be moved, you will need to decide how to manage personal records, which will hopefully have been organized ahead of time. The nursing home will undoubtedly ask for a medical history, medication plan, the names and contact details for physicians, contact information for relatives, and a health directive. They'll also want to know about friends and persons of interest, a brief summary of important events in your elder's life, and who to reach out to in case of an emergency.

Grim as it may be, they will also want to know if you've made arrangements with a funeral home, and for you to designate a person who will come and pick up the elder's belongings and clean out their space when the end comes. Most nursing homes allow a very short timeframe for vacating the premises after a resident passes and the burden to remove items is on you. Needless to say these details are best discussed in private without your loved one present. They will already be dealing with enough as it is.

> "What to bring will be the most challenging question in the days or weeks to come.

During the days or weeks of preparation for the move, be good to yourself and your loved one. Do not forget to include fun or relaxing activities in your schedule once in a while, and try to find ways to help your elder unwind, too – do what you can to take your minds off the big move. Go out to dinner or see a movie. Spend some time alone, or with a friend. You might feel too busy to clear your head or take a break, but it will recharge your batteries and let you come back with renewed focus.

The Days or Months Ahead

The time leading up to the move to a nursing home can be emotionally draining. You might find you have fear, excitement, doubt, sadness, guilt, or conflicting and irrational combinations of all the above.

This is a point where you might get into ugly and unnecessary fights with your elder or other family members simply because everyone is overwhelmed. Before you lash out and say things you might later regret, take six deep breaths. Why six? I'm not sure exactly. I just know it works. The same applies if you are being yelled at for no apparent reason. Remember that everyone's nerves are frayed, but the stress is temporary and your goal is to have your loved one moved safely into a new home.

Once the move arrives, days or even months might have gone by. Boxes will have been packed, and goodbyes said to friends and neighbors. You will have carefully planned the move and prepared both your loved one and yourself for the day. Regardless of how much planning has gone into its smooth execution, though, and how many "ifs and buts" you've crossed off your list, there is one thing you can't plan for – your emotions. The day of the move can take you by surprise. It will unquestionably be the hardest part of your journey.

> *I wasn't prepared for all my own emotions in the weeks leading up to Mom's move to a nursing home, and especially the day of the move itself. I was on a roller coaster. It felt like my insides were being torn apart. I doubted the validity of my decisions and feared I was making a big mistake. All logic had been removed from my mind.*
>
> *As we made the final few preparations to get Mom into her new home, it dawned on me that I had experienced these same feelings before. I remembered my mother dropping me off at kindergarten, only now the roles were reversed. The doubts in my mind were the same I saw on my mother's face when she dropped me off for the first day of kindergarten. She had nodded her head enthusiastically, encouraging me to go inside. Yet her face wasn't all a big smile – I noticed some sadness and confusion. She clearly had a hard time letting go. We both did, I guess, but five minutes later I was playing with my newfound friends and had already forgotten about it. I was just fine.*
>
> *As I recalled those moments, handing my mother over to the nurse who was receiving her, I hoped from the bottom my heart my mother would immerse herself quickly in this new world. I wanted her to be fine, too. I had to trust it would happen.*

It's always difficult when something ends, and especially when we don't know what the future will hold. Fortunately, we can know that change always leaves an opening for a new beginning. The person you love is starting a fresh life. And, they have you to be there with them and help them settle in. You'll be present to make sure they have met their team of caregivers and key administrative personnel, including anyone they will come in contact with on a regular basis (like the cleaning staff). And you can show them the way around the house or facility, not just once but multiple times so they never experience the feeling of being lost.

It is normal for your loved one to feel a little disoriented at first until they know how to navigate their new environment and recognize the many new people around them. Breaking into an established circle of people is hard enough, but things are even more difficult when you're older and most likely not at your best (e.g., signs of stroke). Can you help your elder to make the adjustment? Sure you can.

A few days after my mom moved into the nursing home, I decided to throw a small housewarming party. Everyone was on board, nursing staff and management included. They all thought it was a great idea, and something they hadn't seen before.

My mom was a bit skeptical. She didn't want to draw attention to herself. I wasn't planning a big hoopla, though, just coffee and cake served up with a bit of bubbly (alcoholic and nonalcoholic versions so everyone had a choice). I also bought fun, colorful decorations for the tables and made sure we had enough seating for the residents and the relatives. Not everyone was able to join us, but the ones who did were happy to get acquainted with my mother and me. This little gathering broke the ice for my mom and her new neighbors in a big way.

To this day, the ladies (there were no men there at the time) reminisce about the party. Whenever I visit I get them together for a little re-do – newbies included.

If your loved one is social in nature, the nursing home can provide a great platform to meet people whose life experiences mirror their own. Through social programs they can participate in activities they are passionate about, and even discover new ones, all while making friends.

Unfortunately, not everyone is going to be easy to get along with. Remember the old days, when the chubby kid with thick glasses made fun of you at school? It can happen in nursing homes, too. Some care facilities offer a buddy system for new faces, pairing newcomers with existing residents. Others might use a social worker to help shy residents get acquainted a little more easily. How quickly, and how well, your loved one will make the transition will depend a lot on his or her personality and the people around.

Some nursing homes have assigned seating in the common dining areas. Find out how staff decide where to seat your loved one. It can happen that your senior isn't happy with their pick and that nearby personalities clash. Re-seating can be tricky, and in some facilities they will be hesitant to move a person once a seating order has been established. So, be sure to bring up any concerns early on to get your family member a better place at the table. It's important that your loved one can eat their meals in peace in good company. Be proactive and voice any concerns you have with the facility senior staff members should you suspect any bad behavior from fellow residents, or even from staff. Proper integration is critical for long-term success and happiness.

You and your parent will both need to understand and remember that not everything is going to be perfect from the start. It may take a while before everyone is up to speed, and in the early stages of the move staff might make small mistakes until they have your parent's care and preferences dialed in. This is normal and simply requires a bit of patience from both sides. In the weeks after the move it will be your job to carefully monitor your loved one's behavior and notice any changes or urgent needs.

Should you pick up on any signs of depression – such as a refusal to eat, or difficulty sleeping – talk to the head nurse right away. These can seem like small problems in the beginning, but they could also be indications that something more serious is going on rather than the simple adjustment to a new environment. Assure your parent that you love them and will be watching out and advocating for them while at the same time investigating possible causes of these behavioral changes. In the unfortunate event your parent does not want to remain in the nursing home, you will need to know what your next action will be. The worst-case scenario is for you to pull out Plan B, which you will have arranged in advance.

Let's hope that doesn't happen. I want your loved one to be happy and settle into their new home with few or no problems. That means you have done everything you can to ensure their comfort and can begin to prepare your own return back to normal life. There are just a few more loose ends to tie up before you leave.

Before departing you should agree with your parent in advance on a time when you or other family members will be calling in, or when your loved one can best reach you. Also let the nurses know you will follow up with them on occasion to see if they are noticing any changes in behavior or deterioration of health. Be sure you can obtain critical information via phone, email, or a tool like WhatsApp before you leave. Also be sure the staff has a record of first and secondary points of contacts, usual availabilities, and the best methods to reach you. Advise them of any time differences or other nuances that might factor in.

If you have established a good rapport with the nursing staff you shouldn't have a problem getting information you need over the phone. Just know that even if you call at an agreed-upon time, there's a good chance you will not be able to speak to the nurse you wanted to get on the line. That's especially true if the facility is larger and communication goes through a few layers. Try to work out a system in advance so you can know your messages are being relayed promptly to the right person and you know how you can expect them to respond. You want to set things up so the channels of communication are clear and open at all times. That's easier to arrange when you're on premises than it is when you are hundreds or thousands of miles away.

For over 30 years we had to say goodbye to each other, whether at train stations and airports or in the comfort of home. That was just part of what came with living abroad. It was never easy, but through time we established a little routine. We would hug and then with no further ado I would say: "Okay, let's make it quick. No tears, promise to be good to each other. I love you, I will miss you, and I'll be back soon." And with that I would turn around and roll my luggage out, waving goodbye and blowing a few kisses, and walk away.

The day I departed from Mom's nursing home was slightly different. I had made sure the staff knew I was leaving so they could pay more attention to Mom and keep her busy. In addition, I arranged a "date" with Mom's angel later that afternoon so she couldn't brood. The stage had been set for my departure.

I got ready to do my thing, but when I hugged my mother for the last time tears ran down her face and my throat tightened. "Mom, no tears," I said as I wiped them off her cheek and hugged her a bit harder.

Mom smiled. "I am sorry to see you leave, I got so used to having you around and you have done so much for me. These are tears of joy. I am so happy that you made me such a nice new home and that I am in good hands now. I don't know how to thank you."

I was so glad she told me that. The unbearable thought that I had not done enough was finally lifted. It was a happy ending with tons of hugs, love and deep understanding, and a new beginning at the same time.

At some point, we need to continue living our own lives. When we have done everything we came to do it's time to depart once more. Take your time and get to this chapter on a positive note so both you and your loved one can start anew peacefully. You will both know the work doesn't end here and that you will come back. But for now, pat yourself on the shoulder and go on with your life. It's yours to live.

As time goes on, your parent will feel more at home in their care facility and you will settle into another level of engagement, one that involves supporting everyone involved in your loved one's care from afar.

Reliance and Reassurances

Providing Ongoing Love, Care, and Support

L et's jump forward and look at your life after you've successfully moved your senior into their new home and are returning to your old habits. I suspect your days will probably still feel far from normal, as you may realize again and again that you're in charge of orchestrating the life of another person from a distance. Things will be a bit different now, though, because you are no longer the key player in this game; instead, you'll have a whole team that has taken over for you right where you left off.

It's likely that, from here on out, most of your visits will be over the phone rather than in person. How often you'll be calling will depend on your loved one's health situation and how settled they are into the new facility. You might know instinctively whether phoning daily, twice a week, or once on Sunday afternoon (as examples) is most beneficial for your loved one. If not, you will need to figure out what call intervals are best for yourself, your senior, and the care staff.

These calls may not always be easy, especially in the beginning. Some patients can become very agitated or upset in new surroundings. Your senior may even lash out at you and bitterly blame you for the fact that they are in a nursing home. Keep this in mind and use your best judgment for the best times to have a calm conversation. Don't forget to give yourself (and your loved one) a bit of space when needed.

> *Ever since Mom moved into the nursing home it has become harder for me to get her on the phone. She's constantly busy doing things. You should see her calendar! Breakfast, lunch, coffee, and dinner. In between meals there are activities like bingo and singing, or church and cognitive training. There always seems to be something going on. Even the relatives who live in her time zone have a hard time reaching her.*

Hopefully your loved one is settled in and all parties have begun to perceive the new situation in a positive light, making your interactions meaningful. Over time your topics of conversation might change to reflect the daily events and activities your senior is now a part of. Stay curious about what they describe to you. Listen and get a sense for what their day looks like. Take note of new names and dates that match up to special events. Then you can bring them up the next time you talk with your parent and stay engaged in their life. And, it might be more interesting than you think. You could be surprised about what might happen in a nursing home!

What makes your elder's life worth living? Is there some way you can make them happier? Ask your loved one if they are missing anything. If so, see if you can order and ship it to them. Or, get in touch with staff, or your angel, to see if an issue needs to be resolved. Consider sending an occasional bouquet of fresh flowers to brighten their day, or a new picture of yourself or the grandchildren. These little gestures will make your senior feel supported and remind them they are not forgotten. If you had a routine of doing things for your parent before they moved into the nursing facility, try to keep it going. In other words, do whatever you can to make sure they remain comfortable.

> *To this day, Mrs. G is playing a big role my mother's life. Not only*

does she visit her every Tuesday just as she has for years, but she also makes sure Mom has everything she needs. For example, Mrs. G will swap out Mom's summer and winter clothes and help her keep her closet organized. She buys her fresh fruit or other foods my mother rarely gets from the nursing home kitchen. Right now she is decorating Mom's room for Christmas. We have asked Mrs. G many times to decline if there is something she doesn't want to do, but she has yet to say "no" to spoiling my mom. If we did not have her in our lives my mother's comfort would be seriously curtailed.

The nursing staff can only do so much, meaning the little pleasures of life typically fall to the wayside. This is an unfortunate reality of nursing home living, but one you can help to make up for.

During your conversations with your senior, listen carefully. If he or she is upset about the move, it can happen that they might complain about pretty much *everything*. You need to be able to read between the lines and understand their emotional health is important. You can't be a mind reader, but you can pick up on subtle changes and cues that suggest unusual emotional behavior. Pay attention to signs of serious problems and don't let trivial complaints taint your judgment.

Keep a list of any concerns or questions you have and discuss those items in a timely fashion with the person in charge of your elder's care. Don't forget to follow up, more than once if necessary, to make sure any problems are being addressed. Should you find you can't resolve things by talking with your main point of contact, don't hesitate to go further up the chain of command to be heard.

When it does become necessary to escalate a concern, be thoughtful in the way you communicate. You don't want to ruin your relationship with the caregiver if you can help it, particularly since they play a significant role in supporting your loved one. Also, don't be quick to think that just because you're paying good money for the accommodations and care services you have the right to demand whatever you want. Remain polite and respectful at all times, even if you feel you have good reason to be upset. Your goal should always be to work *with* the caregivers and not *against* them (unless, of course, there is serious misconduct involved).

Many people don't like to think about the realities of life in a nursing home, and don't want to wrap their heads around *any* of it – particularly the inescapable fact that the end of life is approaching. This topic comes into sharper focus when physical or cognitive functions are failing. During these final stages of life, many caregivers will play a big part in the decision-making process as well as providing comfort to your loved one and support to you and your family. You will want to be able to count on them when that time comes, so treat them well.

Use your regular visits with your loved one wisely. Don't hold back on telling your elder how much you love them. Recall the good times you shared together, like the birthday party at the house when the cake smashed to the ground, or the time your brother played a super prank on April Fools' Day. Laugh together and cry together. You don't ever want to have the regret that you didn't tell them all the things you had to say while you still had the chance in their living years.

As humans, all of us are fragile. That makes it extremely difficult to believe you are the cause of someone's suffering. It can wreak havoc on your emotional well-being.

That Nagging Feeling
Dealing with Your Inner Demons and Guilt

Even if you have done everything right for your loved one, you might be haunted by self-doubt or overcome by strong and lasting feelings of guilt after they have been moved into a home. Regardless of how natural and common this tendency to second-guess is – and regardless of how cooperative and well adjusted your loved one is – having these kinds of agonizing thoughts circling through your head is simply awful. Anyone who has had to make these kinds of tough decisions knows what it's like to feel like you have let your parents down or broken some unspoken promise. They are familiar with the shame, anxiety, and sense of loss.

Born during the Depression, a child of World War II, and a survivor of various health scares, my mother has made it to live a long life, with all the ups and downs that entails. She married young, gave birth to my brother and me, and then sacrificed a lot to raise us and give us a better life. Like any good mother she read bedtime stories, cuddled and nursed us when we were sick, and stood up for us when we couldn't stand up for ourselves. Most importantly to me, she stayed strong and was supportive of my decision to leave Germany and find my own life. I am so grateful for her and have always wished I could give something back in the same way.

But how would I ever be able to fill her shoes? If I were to drop everything and move back to my home country to be with her, the consequences would be hard to bear. Was I being selfish? I certainly hoped not. Was I bothered by people perhaps perceiving me as the daughter who was "living the good life in Hawaii" instead of caring for her ailing mother? You bet I was.

To this day, my biggest problem is the feeling of guilt. The emotions come in waves, and have different triggers. Some are self-inflicted, amounting to voices in my head. Others come from conversations with my mother. I've learned to deal with it, for the most part, but I would be lying if I told you I don't still experience those emotions. My therapist keeps telling me I have a right to my own life, and that Mom would only want me to be happy. I know that, of course, but can't help thinking I should be with her.

You might find that you're like me and the "coulda, shoulda, woulda" moments are circling your brain constantly. And just to top it off, there might be the slightest nuance in your loved one's voice – real or imagined – that you believe is criticizing your every decision. Or, if you're one of the unlucky ones, you might even get berated by your otherwise softly spoken elder during every encounter. That doesn't help at all.

Ironically, you may also experience positive feelings. You might have a sense of relief that you'll have more time for yourself, or that your loved one will *finally* be taken care of in a safe place so you don't have to worry so much anymore. Just when that moment comes, and you realize there are a lot of positive aspects of the arrangement to be grateful for, you will probably start to feel guilty again. With all these nasty emotional twists and turns, you can start to feel as if your life is playing out in the wrong movie and that you are constantly looking for the remote to make it stop.

It probably wouldn't surprise you to know that all these conflicting emotions can be harmful to your health. They can weigh you down to the point that even after a good night's sleep you might still feel tired and exhausted during the day. You may be unable to think straight and feel as if you're being pushed to your limit all the time. You might snap at your children or spouse for no apparent reason, or as if you are walking around with a permanent case of PMS. Suffering from caregiver guilt for prolonged periods can even lead to depression in some people.

So, the question faced by many family caregivers, or care organizers, is how to make sense of (and overcome) such troubling thoughts and feelings.

> *For the longest time I wanted to believe it was impossible that my mom might need help. She was always the one who took care of others, but old age finally caught up with her. Macular degeneration is the main cause for her misery; the rest is just a body that is slowly getting weaker due to old age. I take comfort in knowing that nature is the cause of my mother's physical decline, and not something I've done. Whenever I feel guilty about my decisions I try to recognize my emotions for what they really are and allow myself to slowly come to a place of ease.*
>
> *At times when I get really down on myself I turn to what I call my "Three-a-Day Journal." I write down either the last three things I did for Mom, or three things I love about her. This simple activity reminds me that I'm doing the best I can under my circumstances. It also reminds me she is in a safer and better place because of me. It's only by putting things in perspective that I can give myself permission to have a life that isn't totally focused on her.*

As children, and especially daughters, we often have a strong sense of obligation to be there for our parents when they get old and need help. It is a very natural call of duty, and our way to give back. Don't beat yourself over the head if you have the feeling you haven't done enough. Be gentle to yourself and shift your focus and work toward unconditional love to feel better.

If there are lingering unresolved issues or resentments, you should try to reconcile them and put any ill feelings to rest. Otherwise, dealing with guilt over advanced care placement will be a constant inner battle. Getting to a point of acceptance will allow your heart to heal, but first you have to give yourself time and permission to grieve the things that weren't. The past is the past – there is no way of changing it. By acknowledging that fact and reaching a point of acceptance, you allow yourself to find closure and move past old wounds.

Mending what has been broken a long time ago is very hard, and for some older people it's simply not possible in their lifetime. When your parent can't let go of hurts from the past, and keeps pulling off the Band-Aid you have carefully placed on your wounds, you need to establish strict boundaries and steer clear of any conversations that could suck you into old traumas or send you on a guilt trip. Have someone who deeply cares for you remind you that you have a place in their heart, and that they can see how hard you struggle. Let them tell you they see what you are going though and know you're doing your very best under difficult circumstances.

Being able to express those feelings freely to someone you trust, without being criticized or judged, is very important. Find someone you can vent to – not just once, but during the whole ordeal. At times you might sound like a broken record, so the person you use as a sounding board needs to be patient and have a good understanding of what you're going through. Keeping painful emotions inside isn't helpful, and can cause you to lose your cool at the most inopportune moment.

> *For the past four years, I feel like I've kept my calm very well considering all that happened, but there is one particular moment I wish I could take back. After my father passed I took my mom on a trip to a lovely Austrian town for a change of scenery. The accommodations were nice, the food was excellent, and the weather was perfect.*
>
> *It was a gorgeous day as we strolled through this lovely village looking at local crafts and searching for something to eat. I could feel myself getting grumpy. I don't recall exactly what brought it on, but I do remember that at one point I snapped at Mom. It had something to do with the fact*

that she doesn't always hear the phone ring. I was trying to explain to her how she could increase the volume of the ring tone, but she either didn't hear me or didn't want to.

In any event, for whatever reason she kept apologizing for being old. She said it over and over again. I told her that she didn't have to apologize for her age, and that I just wanted to help her with her phone issue, but Mom kept insisting she was not useful for anything and kept on repeating the same tune until I went ballistic. Right there, in the middle of a nice restaurant, I raised my voice and said things that should not have been said.

Mom went quiet. The air was so thick you could cut it with a knife, and her silence exacerbated the heavy cloud that was now hanging over us. We finished our meals without saying anything. When we got back to the hotel I was still very angry – not at her, but at myself. I never would have realized I was hurting her with my technical explanation on how to set up her phone. Instead of reading between the lines I was stuck in problem-solving mode. While I was explaining phone settings, I couldn't hear what Mom was really telling me: that she was sorry to be a burden. I felt awful and wished I could take it all back.

How to Re-set a Shorted Circuit

Getting into the practice of meditation can help immensely with pent-up anger and frustration. When you are guilt tripping and your emotions are going haywire, it's time to give yourself a mental break. Because it can be difficult to recognize when that time has come, it can be good to have someone around who can point out that you have reached the threshold of your patience. You certainly don't want to find out the hard way like I did.

Your loved one is one of millions of people out there who are receiving care in a nursing home. You are doing the best you can, and still arranging for their well-being in a very special way. Just maintaining that perspective can help you deal with guilt and anger. If that's not enough, though, consider finding emotional support through friends, family members, spiritual meditation, or even dedicated support groups. It might feel like no one else understands, but I promise if you sit in on just one or two group therapy sessions you will quickly find you're not alone.

How should we define the perfect living situation for an older, ailing person or younger person with a disability? It depends on who you ask.

Embracing Imperfections
Practicing Patience and Compassion

I f I were to tell you that someone with impaired vision was going to stay in a two-story home all alone, and that it was the perfect situation for them, you might say "no way." But, if you were to watch that same person living in the house – comfortably, because they know every counter, corner, and floorboard – you might get a completely different impression.

You would have been amazed to see my mom's perfectly pressed linens and wonder how she did it. Or to watch her get around the house. She could barely see things, and when she walked she pushed her feet instead of lifting them up. It might have seemed disturbing or dangerous from the outside, but mom was masterfully efficient. It may have taken her a bit longer to get up and down the stairs, but as long as she was in her comfortable environment she did surprisingly well. Take her out of her habitat and put her in a place she had never been before, though, and it was a totally different picture. Suddenly she seemed disoriented. She got uncomfortable and even shaky.

So I had to ask myself: is it possible that we, the able ones, are stuck on what we perceive is the perfect environment? Should we perhaps be challenging our own belief systems and embracing imperfections?

We've all heard it: "Why should I move out of my house? I'm fine." Or, "What's wrong with my chair? You don't like it?" Our old folks can sound like broken records. It frustrates us because we want to make things better for them and know we can. So, when they push back on our suggestions we shake our heads, thinking, "Here we go again. Dad is being difficult," while he stoically plops his butt down in his beloved comfortable but sagging chair.

In these instances it's important to remember that it's not about what we want; it's about what our loved ones want. We shouldn't get ourselves stuck in making things perfect because there isn't any such thing.

Rattling the status quo of an older person, even if it's "for their own good," can give them too much of a good thing. We are all creatures of comfort, and no one likes to have someone come in and mess things up after we've got them the way we like them. The next time you feel compelled to make a change, or to make an improvement for your elder, ask them why they have been doing it the same way for all these years.

Think before you throw out that dusty old piece of kitsch and replace it with something new. It could be that old ceramic doll has sentimental value, or that the frayed blanket Mom likes to snuggle up with reminds her of her late husband. Even if there is no apparent rhyme or reason for the objects they keep, ask yourself: does it really matter? Would you be better off just letting it go and not wasting your energy on things that aren't that important? After all, there are probably more pressing issues that require your attention.

You could apply the same attitude toward conversation. One of the most common signs someone is aged is that they become forgetful. When your parent tells you the same story for the hundredth time cut them a bit of slack. Remember that time is catching up with them. You aren't necessarily speaking to the same person you have known your whole life.

If they become repetitive or stubborn, try taking a step back and changing the subject. Go do something else. Avoid getting stuck in verbal battles, even if you're right, because you won't be able to win. The end result will only be that both of you will become frustrated. The person who is speaking to you might not have the young mind of the loved one you remember. There may be times when you have to ignore or shrug off an insensitive comment. The more defense mechanisms you can incorporate into your interactions with the confused or befuddled elder, the better it will be for everyone involved. This is an area of your life where practicing kindness instead of proving yourself right goes a long way.

Every time I had to go somewhere with Dad I found myself in a predicament. It started when I was a teenager and lasted into adulthood. When we were set to go out I would wonder: should I tell him to change his outfit?

Dad always wore the same type of clothes in the summer: shorts, a plaid shirt, and socks he would pull up high over his sandals. I'm not sure if it was the socks, sandals, or both, but it sure made me feel embarrassed to be seen with him.

As we both got older I became more tolerant of his hideous fashion sense. As I write this, I'm looking at a picture hanging on my office wall of Dad dancing with a Hula girl in Waikiki. The dancer is a gorgeous tanned woman, and my father is standing next to her in his ever-present socks, sandals, and a Hawaiian shirt for the occasion. I absolutely love this photo.

If we got together and started talking about our loved ones' irritating quirks or annoying habits we would end up sitting together past midnight and laughing our pants off. Although we often think of the little things – like my dad's wardrobe – as being cute or funny after the fact, they can easily get in the way of our relationships today. It's almost as if they steal the show. These strange tendencies or behaviors seem to be designed to claim our full attention instead of staying in the background. In some cases, they might even trigger unfortunate responses from us that we later regret.

Have you ever felt embarrassed by your parent or loved one? Have you had the experience of showing up for something like a doctor's visit with your dad while he's wearing his "holey" sweater? Even if you haven't been through that exact ordeal, I bet you can think of a dozen similar ones. We have all been through it: the stares from others, and the times we wish we could crawl into a hole to make ourselves disappear, all because of something a relative did. The next time you find yourself getting angry or impatient with your parent, take a deep breath and smile. It is exactly those quirks that make them adorable. You have to love them for who they are.

> "Raise your hand if you come from a dysfunctional family.

In some cases, the quirks might not be so lighthearted and impossible to shrug off. Not all humans are essentially kind or good-natured, and if you belong to the unfortunate group of people who grew up in an abusive or neglectful environment and never had good relationships with your family members, you might have to make some hard decisions. Maybe you will be the one taking on the role of care organizer for your parent and maybe you won't, but ultimately you will probably be involved one way or the other. Be prepared for the possibility that your elder will be pushing your buttons during every single encounter, or will create a toxic environment. Just do your best to remind yourself that they are reaching the end of their journey and you need to get through it. Prepare for a tough time and commend yourself for giving it a shot.

From dealing with a person who is just unpleasant to be around to arranging care for a sick and abusive person (for example, a raging alcoholic), make sure you understand what you're getting yourself into. It might be that you have never had a healthy relationship with this person. That might not even be your fault. This might be the time to acknowledge and accept that some things will never change. It doesn't mean you or your senior family member can't make amends, but repairing a deeply scarred relationship will require a ton of work on both sides.

Sadly, deeply manifested psychological disorders are so multifaceted that the constant aggravation they cause can lead to all kinds of health issues – both for the elder and the care organizer. Dealing with these kinds of complicated issues is beyond my competence and the scope of this book, but I will offer what I consider to be a solid piece of advice: *don't go it alone.* Engage a counselor during this time and know when to walk away if things aren't working out. When a situation becomes unbearable or dangerous, it's better to leave it to the pros to organize personal care.

Relationships are complicated and we are all human, for better or worse. As much as you might find your senior's habits annoying, irritating, or worse, getting upset about it won't help anyone. Constant aggravation can cause all kinds of health issues, and getting stressed over things you cannot change helps no one. Safety and comfort for your elder should be your main considerations – everything else is icing on the cake.

Laugh often when dealing with the person you care about and find your own ways of embracing imperfections. Follow the guidance of the famous serenity prayer and know when to let go of things you simply aren't able to change.

My dad entertaining the crowd – priceless.

Recognize the signs that lead to burnout and do something just for yourself. Listen to music, take a bath, or meet a friend. Don't think twice about this – it's all right.

Taking a Breather

Avoiding Burnout and Caring for Yourself

Everywhere you look, people are struggling with stress. The term burnout shows up so frequently, from dinner conversations to high-level medical studies, that it is easy to tell how deeply it plagues our society.

When you add the burden of organizing care for someone you love to the daily grind you are already facing, it's easy to find yourself so completely stressed out that you end up in the doctor's office. By trying to do the noble thing and care for others, we often set aside our own needs. We aim to become the perfect son or daughter – on top of being the perfect husband, wife, father, mother, and professional – and fail to care for ourselves in the process.

Some people might tell you how rewarding it is to give back to your elders, and it certainly can be. Unfortunately, it can also lead to burn-out very quickly.

It's 4:15 AM. All of a sudden an unexpected voice wakes me. Mom sits on my bed blabbering away. "The physical therapist said yesterday I need to get a new cast for my elbow. So I decided to stay home today, not go to adult day care. Maybe I can get a new cast."

"Mom, what are you doing here?" I asked. "How did you get up the stairs by yourself, and what are you talking about? Why a new cast? Do you even know what time it is?"

Mom just kept going. "The driver probably won't come to pick me up today, or will he?"

I pull myself together, determined not to yell at her in the middle of the night. Instead, I say: "You're making no sense. Of course you're going to day care. The driver will come to pick you up as scheduled, and our doctor's appointment is in two weeks. That's when the cast will be removed. Come on, let's go back to bed. It's very early."

Mom mumbles, "Yes, dear," and five minutes later she is fast asleep. Of course, I'm wide awake – and feeling grouchy! No wonder, with just two hours of shut-eye…

There is a good chance you can identify with this situation. I know it's nothing compared to the trials and tribulations caregivers of patients with severe disabilities like Alzheimer's go through, but these kinds of episodes weren't making my life any easier. Eventually, a lack of sleep combined with the constant reminders that your loved one is going through physical and mental decline *will* get to you. Being fearful of further decline, and holding on to accompanying feelings of helplessness, can bring you to your knees. You may find yourself inching mentally and emotionally closer to a breaking point.

Burnout can happen anywhere, and to anyone. When you are away from home the odds are stacked a little more heavily against you because you're not acting in your natural environment. If you are usually a physically active person, for example, and now are spending most of your time tending to others, running errands, and negotiating someone else's life, without getting the exercise you are used to, your body will start to rebel. You will bear the consequences, and possibly more quickly than you think.

As soon as you experience physical discomfort or pain in your body,

you need to take precautions and address them with proper maintenance and care. Don't ignore warning signs like joint pain, abdominal
pain, headaches, insomnia, or depression. In each case your body is
telling you to do something about your current situation. It is signal-
ing to you that you are reaching (or have already reached) your limit
and it's time to take a breather.

It's easy to fall into the trap of thinking you don't have time for doctors' visits because your plate is too full. But you won't help anyone by
putting yourself in a position where you're out of commission physically or not mentally strong enough to deal with new challenges. If you
want to organize care for your family member, you need to be focused
and ready. This is not the right time to put your own health on the
back burner and make excuses for not seeking out help. Caring for
your senior is like being on an airplane: you have to secure your own
mask before you can assist others.

Typical Burnout Symptoms

- Emotional exhaustion
- Cynicism
- Feeling ineffective
- Frequent colds or sicknesses
- Headaches
- Insomnia
- Depression
- Anxiety
- Tendency to alleviate stress in unhealthy ways
  (alcohol, drugs, shopping)

When you experience long periods of sleeplessness or outright de-
pressive moods, it's time to consult a physician to get help. Unresolved
issues can have serious health consequences.

According to Amelia and Emily Nagoski from the book *Burnout*:

"Stress is the neurological and physiological shift that happens in your body when you encounter [stressors]"... i.e., an internal response. Typical stressors are external, such as financial problems, existential worries, working on endless tasks, or caring for the sick without a break (even organizing care for a loved one). Plenty of books provide self-help guidance on how to deal with stress. Yet, when we are trying to fix burnout it can feel as if you are simply adding more stressors to the equation. The result is that we don't even try to fix it.

Rarely do we recognize that this is a pattern that can be rewritten and gently changed. There are ways to fight the state of emotional, physical, and mental exhaustion. Ultimately, putting them to work helps everyone involved.

> *I happen to like to surf and play tennis. Surfing is a very solemn sport. When I am lying on my board I feel connected to the elements. My thoughts just drift when I paddle out into the waves. It happens naturally and I don't resist it. When I am happy I smile and when I am sad I let my tears flow. No one can see them anyway. On the tennis court I just swing my racket as hard as I can to get all my frustrations out. I also laugh together with my teammates over silly mis-hits. Allowing myself to indulge in these activities has been a lifesaver for me. And, as a bonus, I have gotten pretty good at them.*

Manage Your Time

You can't take care of yourself if you don't make room in your schedule. If you have time-management issues those need to be addressed before anything else in your life. Go back to the chapter **Get Your Ducks in a Row** for my suggestions on how to better manage the hours in your day.

Exercise

Try to find half an hour per day or more to do some form of physical activity. It could be a run in the park, a bike ride, or anything else you enjoy. When you can, exercise outdoors. That lets you kill two birds with one stone – you are getting your heart rate up *and* spending some time in nature. Both are great for your mental state. Break a sweat and let the happy endorphins do the rest for you. You'll feel better almost immediately, and might even get a more restful night's sleep.

Sleep

For many of us, the idea of getting eight to ten hours of uninterrupted sleep per night amounts to wishful thinking. But make no mistake: you do need your rest. Insomnia is one of the most persistent struggles for busy people, and we now know it can lead to all kinds of more serious problems. A lack of sleep has been associated with cardiovascular disease, cancer, Alzheimer's, and other ailments. Bad sleep compounds into bad moods, poor nutrition, and worse health.

> *Lights out, pajamas on, and into bed. As soon as my head hits the pillow I'm drifting off into a deep sleep – partly because it was another long day filled with work and lengthy conversations with my mother.*
>
> *Around 2:30 AM I find I'm wide awake. A gazillion thoughts are racing through my head. My brain seems to function better at night than it does during the day. I find I can solve difficult problems, even though the solutions have disappeared in the morning no matter how hard I try to remember them.*
>
> *I'm well aware that tossing and turning won't help anything, but still I try to get back to sleep. I start counting backward from 1,000... By the time I reach 569, still awake, I give up and make a cup of tea. I head into the other bedroom to read. If it's an easy, entertaining book I know I'll be back asleep within twenty to sixty minutes on average.*
>
> *When the next morning comes I oversleep my alarm. Darn, I'm late for work. I drink down my coffee, wolf down breakfast, and rush to the office. My brain feels like mush. I know this can't be good. Probably tonight will be better, but then the next night will be worse again. It's a rinse-and-repeat process. I wonder: how in the world am I going to break this vicious cycle?*

Knowing how much harm a lack of sleep can cause should give you more reason to try to get enough shut-eye. A good night's sleep literally recharges your batteries.

There are a few things you can do to create a good environment for sleep. Rule number one: use your bedroom only for sleep and sex. Rule number two: keep your bedroom free of any electronic devices, blinking or blue lights, etc. And rule number three: the room should be dark and the temperature slightly on the cool side.

Those three rules are the most important for getting solid rest. There are, of course, a whole lot of other things you can do to create the perfect conditions for a good night of sleep. It's also worth noting that paying attention to proper nutrition and exercise is just as important to the quality of your sleep as having your bedroom set correctly. For instance, drinking caffeinated beverages and eating heavy carb-loaded meals late in the day can disrupt your sleep patterns. So can dosing your worried mind with alcohol. One beer or single glass of wine might be fine, but once you indulge in more booze than that you can say goodbye to your hope of sleeping soundly.

If you spend more than twenty minutes in bed and your mind is still racing, it's best to get up and move into a dimly lit room. Don't touch your phone or iPad, even if you have them set to sleep mode. It's not important to know what time it is or what you might have missed in the last couple of hours. You want to quiet your mind, not agitate it more. Write down your thoughts on a notepad and then finish by writing down, "These things can wait until tomorrow." You've given yourself permission to put things aside until they're dealt with later, which makes it easier to go back to bed for round two.

If you're still experiencing insomnia after rearranging your bedroom, cleaning up your lifestyle, and trying these exercises you might want to speak to your doctor to rule out any medical conditions. They may even refer you to a sleep specialist who can help.

Meditate and Try Yoga

If you can't spare 30+ minutes for an exercise session, you should consider doing some meditation or yoga. You can try either in as little as ten minutes. Finding time for reflection isn't always easy, but it can be incredibly healing to give your mind some rest.

Many of us instinctively turn to medication instead of meditation when dealing with anxiety or busy thoughts, but I've found mindful activities to be a better solution than pills. That's because they teach you to clear your mind without side effects, and to cope with problems instead of symptoms.

Getting started is easy, and there are many meditation apps available. Personally, I use Headspace®, which has a trial version you can download to your phone. The paid version with more features is available in the app store.

Just like meditation, you can do yoga in the comfort of your own home, shaving off valuable time that would have been spent driving to a gym or studio. Just plop down your mat, do some downward dog asanas, and feel your energy start flowing.

"But," you say, "I'm already stretched too thin. How could I *possibly* carve out time for these personal extravagances?" Keep reading...

Breathe!

Let's say you can't even carve ten minutes out of your schedule, or don't have a quiet place for yoga or meditation. How about breathing?

As much as we love our elders, there are going to be times when they drive us crazy. One way to avoid going nuts is to avoid the "hooks" and breathe. Deeply. To see how this works, tune into one of my favorite simple five-minute breathing exercises on YouTube. You can find it by visiting YouTube and searching "Stacey Schuerman breathe." The great thing about that video is it gives you a five-minute break and doesn't require you to go anywhere or do anything special. It's just breathing, and it works.

Daydream

Another stress-busting fix you can put to use anytime is simply letting your mind wander without interference. It doesn't matter where you are (unless you're behind the wheel), you can simply let your thoughts drift.

You might think you do this already. And, some people say that they use computers and social media to take their minds off of more serious issues. Daydreaming is different, and in my opinion more effective than screen time. In fact, I would argue that the opposite is probably true, and that setting boundaries on screen time probably helps to reduce your stress levels.

Staring at clouds in silence, on the other hand, and imagining faces or animal shapes in the sky is a much better way to quiet your thoughts and reset your mind. Likewise, when you are at the park watching children play and dogs fetch sticks, your thoughts linger on what you observe. Daydream and savor sweet moments. It's something you can do at any time or place, and as you make it a habit you'll notice, appreciate, and intensify the positive aspects of your life.

Find Creative Outlets

Not everyone is an artist, but if you take pleasure in drawing, painting, writing, or even playing an instrument, then try to spend some time doing something imaginative and pleasurable. The act of creating something can be very therapeutic and can force us to challenge ourselves in fun ways. Finding a creative outlet can be soothing, while at the same time allowing you to shift your focus toward something completely unrelated to the problems that were on your mind.

To beat stress and stretch your mind, make some time to let your creative juices flow in whatever direction they want to take.

Maintain Positive Social Connections

A good hug can't be beat. And when you're stressed, it's the best medicine for your soul.

Touch and social connections have a positive impact on our health. Being with others we care for, and who care for us, can lower anxiety, push away depression, and allow us to express greater empathy toward others. Each of these positive feelings improves our physical and emotional health.

Whether it's getting together with a friend for lunch, snuggling up with a spouse, or just cuddling with a pet, there are many ways to feel in touch with those around you. In times of distress it just feels good to be able to let go of any worries and lean on someone's shoulder and be heard without being criticized or judge. Savor it – however brief the moment.

Make Time for You

We all know we should be taking better care of ourselves, but most of us don't. Usually it's because we think we don't have the time. So just in case you are thinking that none of the above is ever going to happen, pause for a moment and start thinking about *how* you'll carve out some valuable minutes to go for a run, make a painting, or steal a hug.

My recommendation is to put your skepticism aside and learn about the Tiny Habit Method®.

The approach is fairly straightforward. You simply add something new to an activity you already do on a daily basis. For example, let's hope you brush your teeth in the morning and in the evening. If you wanted to incorporate yoga or meditation into your day you could do it right before or after you brush your teeth. This is just a simple example; you could certainly come up with your own.

The thought behind this system is simple: it's easier to add a new habit to an existing one, especially if the new habit only extends the old one by a short period of time. If, on the other hand, you're trying to fit the new habit into your already busy schedule without an anchor, there would be a good chance life would get in the way and you wouldn't ever get to it.

I didn't invent this concept, of course. There's a whole book written about it. Check out Tiny Habits: Small Changes That Change Everything by BJ Fogg, Ph.D. (visit: **tinyhabits.com**)

> *Here's how I got started doing yoga: every morning after setting up the coffee maker and feeding the animals, I roll out my mat. While the coffee maker is coming on in the background, I am slowly breathing in and breathing out. My morning ritual is a result of gradually incorporating this new habit. If I had tried to go for too much, like driving half an hour to attend a yoga class somewhere, I most likely wouldn't have stuck with it. It's not that I don't like yoga classes – I do – but that it's so much easier for me to keep the habit up at home and not spend valuable time on the road.*

This method works incredibly well, and I hope you'll give it a try. Before you know it you might be chanting *namaste*, or playing your instrument again, on a regular basis.

Whatever method you use, taking a breather once in a while is critical to keeping your sanity. You have to stay on top of your own health and well-being, especially during the challenging part of your life when you take on the task of looking after an elder. You don't want to let care organizing take over your life and cause irreversible harm to your mental or physical health. I'm sure your loved one would agree with me on that.

Epilogue

Reflections

Writing this book has been much harder than I had anticipated. It wasn't only because English isn't my mother tongue, or that I had never written a book before. Mostly it was because I had to relive parts of the past which brought back to mind some upsetting moments. The road had been pretty rocky at times and, looking back, there were things I could've done better. My patience had been tested on many occasions and I was not always the kind of person I would have liked to have been. I also could have been easier on myself and others. If I have caused hurt feelings to the people in my life, I hope they know I'm sorry.

I have also come to realize that my family's situation is fairly *easy* compared to other more complicated ones. Family relationships can be screwed up in ways I haven't experienced. There are illnesses much more devastating than the ones my parents have gone through, and some adult children face the issues I have at much earlier points in their lives. Moreover, the German health care system covers more costs than the American system does, resulting in less financial strain on families. However, even then the quality of care depends largely on the luck of the draw, regardless of where you live.

There is no doubt in my mind that I have been lucky. Things have worked out pretty well for my mother and myself. I feel blessed to have people who love and support me wherever I go – whether I'm recalled back to Germany or setting foot at home on American soil. Sometimes, at the end of one of my transatlantic trips, I find myself wondering whether my next long journey will be for a vacation or a more serious reason, but then I catch myself. I refuse to go there in my mind because I'd rather focus on today. I hope you will, too.

The days of our lives, for all of us, are numbered. And yes, there are certainly times when we aren't able to muster as much strength and patience as we would like. It's called being human.

Afterthought

What Will the Future Hold?

As I finish this manuscript, the world is under lockdown due to the coronavirus pandemic.

We are living in unprecedented times that no one could have possibly anticipated. My mom's nursing home in Germany is doing an amazing job keeping the residents safe, and I'm counting my blessings. It isn't easy for my mother being locked up in a small room, of course, or to have limited interactions with other residents. But she is handling it with grace and determination.

We talk daily on the phone, and during our visits I play a few songs on the guitar. We speak about the good old times and laugh often. Humor is a good coping mechanism for both of us. Of course it crosses my mind once in a while that having her in a nursing home comes with a unique set of dangers right now, but when I consider what the alternative would be her current living arrangement wins every time. So far, her facility is doing the best they can handling the COVID cases. I'm not sure Mom would have been able to avoid it on her own.

I couldn't be more grateful for the love and care the staff is extending to my mother every day, and for Mrs. G – our angel – who is still looking after Mom and replenishing her goodies to keep her spirit alive. Knowing that my she is safe and cared for is a huge relief.

I don't know what the future will bring, but I feel hopeful Mom will stay safe and happy. When I think about all that's happened over the past year, I have to ask myself: Who would have thought that all my preparation would pay off in such a big and unexpected way?

Acknowledgements
Many Thanks – Mahalo – Dankeschön

Becoming a care organizer unexpectedly might have been the biggest challenge I have faced in my life. Writing my first book (in my second language) was a close second. Luckily, it wasn't something I had to do all at once or completely on my own. There are so many people who helped me bring my dream to life, and who kept me moving forward when the project seemed overwhelming. My deepest thanks go to:

Cindie, you are such a good friend and my favorite sounding board. I couldn't have done this without your patience and feedback. Your firsthand experience about providing care for someone with Macular Degeneration helped me so much during my journey. Julia, your friendship and input from the perspective of a senior care provider were invaluable. Heather, thank you for being such a wonderful friend and using your experience in the publishing world to help me get my book into print. I just wish we lived closer. Rhonda, a big *Mahalo* (thank you) for making time in your busy schedule. Your expert review of basic elder law made this book more complete. BK, thank you for always offering an open ear during the ups and downs of my journey, and also for providing me with your unbiased academic viewpoint when needed. Karen, thanks for being a friend, for serving so many seniors in your career, and for sharing your perspectives with me. Claire, your firsthand experience of providing care for your mother helped me find questions and ideas that weren't obvious when I started writing. Sigi, you are my steady rock on the other side of this globe. Without your initial encouragement this project would have never become reality.

As promised the first signed copy of this book is yours. Matt, thanks for helping me to smooth out the rougher points of English grammar and for never dropping the ball on me during the stressful times of COVID. Jeanne, thank you for being a wonderful part of my family and my life. And to John, my love, soulmate, best friend, and partner of almost 20 years, for putting up with me spending endless hours on this project. I'm so glad you have been with me on this great adventure, and your encouragement meant everything.

My deepest apologies to anyone I might have missed. I promise any oversights weren't intentional. This has been a long and challenging process (but a rewarding one). I've learned along the way just how important it is to have the right friends and resources in your life. I hope you will all accept my love and gratitude for the part you have played in helping me to create the book you just read.

Made in the USA
Las Vegas, NV
08 May 2021